Richard A. Walker is Professor Emeritus of Geography at the University of California, Berkeley. He has written on a diverse range of topics in geography. His books include *The Capitalist Imperative* (1989), *The New Social Economy* (1992), *The Conquest of Bread* (2004), and *The Country in the City* (2007). He is currently working on books on the history and geography of the Bay Area and the political economy of California.

Suresh K. Lodha is Professor of Computer Science at the University of California, Santa Cruz. He is interested in curating, analyzing, and visualizing data for personal empowerment, public policy, and social change. He is a coauthor of *The Atlas of Global Inequalities* and has published more than 100 articles in journals and in conference proceedings.

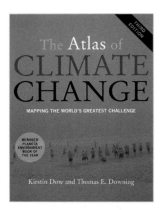

In the same series:

"Unique and uniquely beautiful. . . . A single map here tells us more about the world today than a dozen abstracts or scholarly tomes." — *Los Angeles Times*

"A striking new approach to cartography. . . . No one wishing to keep a grip on the reality of the world should be without these books." — *International Herald Tribune*

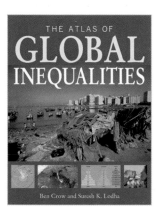

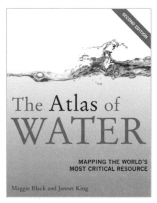

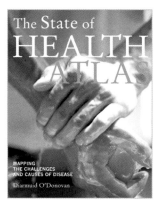

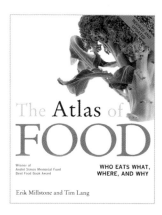

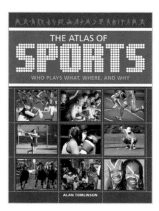

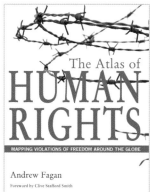

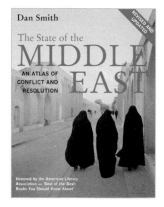

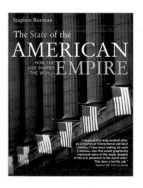

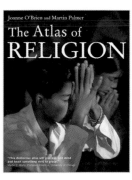

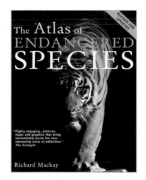

The Atlas of
CALIFORNIA

MAPPING THE CHALLENGES OF A NEW ERA

Richard A. Walker and Suresh K. Lodha

UNIVERSITY OF CALIFORNIA PRESS

Berkeley   Los Angeles

University of California Press, one of the most distinguished university presses in the United States, enriches lives around the world by advancing scholarship in the humanities, social sciences, and natural sciences. Its activities are supported by the UC Press Foundation and by philanthropic contributions from individuals and institutions. For more information, visit www.ucpress.edu.

University of California Press
Berkeley and Los Angeles, California

Library of Congress Control Number: 2013939442
ISBN: 978-0-520-27202-6 (pbk. : alk. paper)

Produced for University of California Press by
Myriad Editions
Brighton, UK
www.MyriadEditions.com

Edited and coordinated by Jannet King
Designed by Isabelle Lewis
Additional design by Corinne Pearlman
Maps and graphics created by Isabelle Lewis

Printed on paper produced from sustainable sources.
Printed and bound in Hong Kong through Lion Production
under the supervision of Bob Cassels, The Hanway Press, London.

17 16 15 14 13
10 9 8 7 6 5 4 3 2 1

CONTENTS

Chapter One LAND & PEOPLE 16

Chapter Two POLITICS, GOVERNANCE, & POWER 30

Chapter Three ECONOMY & INDUSTRY 42

INTRODUCTION

California is just a sliver of the globe, a slice off the west coast of North America, one state among many United States; but it is more, much more. California is a world apart, a region unto itself, a state within a state, a place with its own character. New York, Washington DC, and Texas all feel very far away in outlook and obsessions. If, as a famous coffee company's slogan has it, "geography is a flavor", then California is one of the most distinctive and full-bodied.

To draw up an atlas of California requires considerable imagination. It is a hard state to get one's head—and compass—around. This is about more than its slightly crooked torso and varied landforms. It is about more than geographic subregions that so shape the life and outlook of residents, dividing Northern and Southern Californians at the Tehachapis, urbanites west of the Coast Ranges from farmers in the interior, or rainforest dwellers on the North Coast from desert denizens by the Salton Sea. It is about the way human history is deeply imprinted on the landscape in the form of gargantuan cities climbing the foothills of the San Gabriels, mines and tailings in the Sierra foothills, and farms stretching for miles across the Imperial Valley. The human geography of California is sometimes plainly evident, as in roads and skyscrapers, but sometimes obscure, like the toil of farmworkers or the quality of schools. A critical task of an atlas such as this is to make visible key facets of the human landscape of this great state.

Because it is a place apart, California is rife with myths. One of the most persistent is that it is "The Coast", a place of hippies and stars, not to be taken too seriously; yet what happens here is of crucial importance to the country, and sometimes the world. One reason is that California is not the mythic land of sun and surf, a place of leisure, but a center of industry, technology, and work. As a result, it is not the afterthought of the manufacturing Midwest or the New South, but the principal motor of the American economy. Another persistent myth is that people come to California for its balmy climate and decide to stay, rather than be drawn by jobs on offer by that economy, by the desire to rejoin distant friends and families, or by the need to escape dangers at home.

Californians' favorite origin myths dwell on the misty realms of the past. In Northern California, pride of place is held by the legend of the Gold Rush, with the hardy pioneers of 1849 facing adversity but finding gold aplenty (carried away by picturesque Wells Fargo stagecoaches). From this comes the moniker, The Golden State. Even though the easy gold ran out quickly, the Gold Rush is still seen recapitulated in every boom time from Comstock Silver to Silicon Valley. The Southern California origin myth is different, since the Gold Rush barely touched the region. Instead, the tale oft told is that of the civilizing role of the Spanish Missions, which enter the state from the south. The Mission Dream is embodied in plays and movies, but especially in the colonial revival architecture of the early 20th century which embellishes cities from Santa Barbara to Riverside. Astonishing as it may seem, California school children still have their impressionable heads filled up with these "just-so" stories in the required year of state history doled out in the 4th grade. Worse, they are likely never to get another lesson about what transpired after those founding moments of modern California—let alone what might be just plain wrong with these idyllic pictures of the state's history.

The most popular myth of all is undoubtedly the California Dream, which means anything and everything that people might imagine about their futures—and hence nothing solid at all. It is invoked to explain everything from farm settlement to postwar suburbs. Californians have had many dreams, and some have come true; but the real question is why dreams succeed or why they fail. If the California Dream has a germ of truth, it must be based on political economic realities, not merely the fantasies of literature, cinema, or theater.

In this atlas, we eschew the usual myths for a more hard-nosed look at the Golden State, its successes and failures, its past and present, its human and natural contours. The real building blocks of California's success have been the wealth of nature, an abundance of labor, and economic innovation, backed by a strong measure of good government. California has had the great luck, owing to its physical geography, to be sitting on mountains of gold and silver, great pools of oil, fast-moving rivers, thick forests, and some of the best farmland on earth—not to mention a favorable climate for growing things. The Gold Rush myth rests on this natural abundance, which went far beyond placer deposits, and which ended up back in Sacramento and San Francisco where it could be spent and invested on industrial development and urban expansion. Neither Spanish padres nor Anglo health-seekers after the sun had much to do with the growth of Los Angeles: oil and citrus launched modern Southern California. Even movies and aircraft came later. California grew out of its land, first of all, as we note in Chapter 1.

California has benefited equally from the wealth of labor it drew in, and the aspirations of this ever-plentiful stream of people have been key to the idea of the California Dream. And, yes, folks came here full of hope, but they also came bearing valuable skills and heads full of knowledge and new ideas. Their payoff was good, too, and not just for the winners and stars. Coming to the Golden State worked out well for millions of the ordinary folk who built the cities and farms, laid down roads and levees, and manufactured cars and tractors. Yes, there were geniuses like Lee DeForest and Steve Jobs, but most people contributed by hard work, an improvement here and there, and acting as part of teams with collective dreams. Hence, Chapter 1 shows the land filling with people, who came in waves that broke our California's shores, creating an amazing diversity unlike anywhere in the USA or even the world. With them came a dream of a mingled humanity from every continent that continues to this day.

California has also been one of the great economic success stories in human history, and it has grown by leaps and bounds. Success in a capitalist world economy is never a static thing; it demands endless self-renewal by companies, nations, and regions. This endless renewal and growth has been the third foundation of the California Dream. The wealth of labor had to be put to work: producing more output, creating and using new machines, developing new industries, planting and processing new kinds of crops, designing and building new highways and houses, and more. Chapter 3 provides some windows on this process.

California has been a technological hot-house. The developments here of pumps, nozzles, drills, and more, revolutionized global mining in the 19th century and later the oil industry. The state also invented modern agribusiness, based on food processing, massive dams, and modern fertilizers. It became an industrial powerhouse, surpassing the Midwest as the frontier of American genius, just as the latter had previously surpassed New England. Hollywood created new cameras, color film and sound, as well as the studio and star systems. LA aircraft companies designed single-wing planes, jet engines and mass assembly. Bay Area inventors came up with the vacuum tube, loudspeaker and television—all long before Silicon Valley.

New things introduced in California have spread far and wide, changing the world. Some of these are everyday tools like the computer mouse and windows invented in Palo Alto, or the Google search engine, brain child of two Stanford students. Some are closely identified with California, like the fiberglass surfboard, while others, like the Zamboni ice resurfacer, are a surprise. Some are high tech, such as guidance systems for NASA rockets, while others are cultural, such as the Berkeley coffee-bar model copied by Starbucks.

The economic fertility of California is not principally a matter of soil or sunshine, but of cities. California is a highly urbanized state and cities are the principal arenas of economic growth in the modern era. Cities are where capital, labor, and trade are concentrated, where new ideas are most likely to blossom and bear fruit. Indeed, today the very largest metropolitan regions are outgrowing smaller cities around the world. As shown in Chapter 4, Los Angeles set the pace throughout the 20th century, and greater LA has never stopped growing, swallowing everything in its path. San Francisco had a meteoric rise of its own in the 19th century, dominating the Pacific Coast, and the Bay Area remains one of the country's largest urban regions. San Diego and Sacramento are major cities in their own right, but one can hardly tell any more where one urban area ends and the next begins along the South Coast or Central California.

California's infrastructure, from highways to electrical grids, is another of its great achievements, and one that marks the landscape so strongly that it merits extended treatment in Chapters 4 and 5. Energy supply is the crux of the matter, a foundation for economic and urban growth and deeply implicated in potential disasters to come from rampant climate change. Cities and buildings, highways and ships, water supply and farms are the major arenas of energy use, and hence key targets for California's efforts to develop new energy policies and technologies to cope with global warming. The state will not be able come to grips with climate change, however, without altering profoundly Californians' ways of doing things, from driving to drinking, and these changes are likely to demand a radical reworking of California's infrastructure and the landscape depicted in this atlas.

California's success is about more than innovation and industry, of course. It is a political achievement in which people have fought for their principles and their well-being, for better and more helpful government programs, and to keep the doors open to new generations and new ideas. Politics and government appear here in Chapter 2, but matters of political concern, public policy, and government run through all the chapters of this volume. Politically, California owes much of its success to popular movements that changed the face of the state, and ultimately shaped its people, economy, and geography. These movements include struggles by workers and unions to maintain good pay and benefits; by suffragists to open up democratic participation, and by women for comparable-worth wages; by Chinese and Japanese protective organizations to resist anti-Asian racism and cruelty; by African American and Chicano civil rights campaigners to end school, housing, and employment segregation; by the disabled and homosexuals to liberate society from ancient prejudices; and by too many others to recount here. Even though this is not an historical atlas, it does provide some key background facts that explain how California has come to be what it is today.

Because of the efforts of its people to carve out political and geographic space for everyone to live more fruitful lives, California became a more civilized place. It went from a raw and bleeding frontier to a civilization of a special kind: one that sought to provide a good education for all, a fair shake for working people, a decent retirement and healthcare for everyone, a racially impartial society, and much more. California became a model of enlightened governance in the postwar era, known for its social liberalism as compared with most of the Cold War United States. It still stands out in some regards today, as in the striking majorities won by President Obama in 2008 and 2012, as noted in Chapter 2; or in the rapid adoption of ObamaCare provisions by the state and its forward-looking treatment of preschoolers, as discussed in Chapter 7.

But the political history of California is by no means entirely a shining tale of progress and justice. On the contrary, there is a dark side to the state's history, full of failure, suffering, conflict, murder, even genocide. This is why perpetuating the myth of the California Dream does more than mislead us as to the origins of California's success; it does serious harm by obscuring the damage done to the land, the people and the commonweal by those without scruples, social controls, or thought for tomorrow. The brutal face of California is first revealed in the terrible fate of the Native Peoples, discussed in Chapter 1. It continues through such nasty epochs as Chinese exclusion, alien land laws, and Philippine conquest, and thence to Japanese internment in World War II, exploitation of Bracero "guest workers", beating of farm labor organizers, and blaming "illegal aliens" for budget shortfalls.

Not everyone has shared in the California Dream. Racism has often served a useful purpose for those who benefitted from the dominant position of White people. Miners profited from the slave labor of natives, Irish benefitted from tighter labor markets incurred through boycotts of Chinese workers, and Okies were able to move to the cities when Braceros were imported to do farm work. Even clearer are the benefits won by upper-class Whites, by such means as paying lower wages to "colored labor", eliminating Japanese farmers as competitors, creating exclusive residential areas in cities and suburbs, and more. The misuse of power has been a repeated theme in California history, from the state's birth as a child of colonialism to its 20th century role as a military launchpad for American wars and adventures around the world. If the Spanish empire left traces in crumbling missions, a few presidios and many lovely place names, while the Russians left only a single site, Fort Ross, the American empire continues to leave a deep imprint on California geography. This has been the most militarized of all the states, as shown in Chapter 2. Militarized crime control has left its mark, as well, in the Golden Gulag of prisons and jails across the state, and a more subtle one on the legal codes, the make-up of the judiciary, and lives of millions of young men of color.

These tangible geographies of power are closely linked to California politics, as well. The state was a leader in the neo-conservative wave of the last two generations (often called, confusingly, "neo-liberalism"). California sent Ronald Reagan to the White House in 1980, along with half his cabinet, where they presided over a political revolution, one that dismantled much of the New Deal/Social Welfare state in the US and introduced a new set of principles based on freeing up markets, cutting taxes and shrinking government, and letting the successful get richer and the unsuccessful fend for themselves. California led the pack in many of the key domains of neo-conservative policy: the wars on crime and drugs, deregulating banks and finance, and building up the border wall between the US and Mexico. Most famously, it gave birth to the "tax revolt" with Proposition 13 in 1978, among other revenue-reducing accomplishments.

The effects of these political shifts on government, budgets, and incarceration are detailed in Chapter 2. State and local governments in California have been hovering on bankruptcy for 30 years, and several cities and school districts have tipped over the edge. For years the parties, the legislature and the governor's office have been deadlocked and ineffective, while too many of the enlightened features of California's postwar civilization have eroded: schools, universities, pensions, healthcare, safety, housing—and, one might say, even humanity towards one another.

This comes at the worst time possible, just as the state needs to cope with the education of millions of young people of color—the legacy of mass immigration to feed the booming labor markets of the 1970s and 1980s. The schools and colleges are bursting at the seams at the same time as they are having their budgets slashed, making it that much harder for young people to get a good education. On top of this, healthcare costs in California, as throughout the US, have skyrocketed, weighing heavily on the budgets of households, corporations, and governments trying to care for the sick and aged. But the state is not doing the job it should in seeing to it that all its citizens are adequately insured or that they have sufficient pensions to live out their days without want, as discussed in Chapters 7 and 8.

Today, the shine has gone off the Golden State. So it is more important than ever to take the mythology of California's blessings and success with a grain of salt. There is a sense of fading glory, despite the gloss of iPhones and Oscars. On the whole, the California economy has stumbled into the 21st century, despite the fame of Silicon Valley and Hollywood and the billions racked up by high tech and entertainment giants like Apple and Disney.

California has created too few new jobs for too long, and it absolutely cratered in the Great Recession, with over 2 million workers unemployed and some of the highest unemployment rates in the country, whether measured by state, county, or metropolitan area. This was the vortex of the housing bubble, with more price inflation and bad loans than any other state, ending with a crash that left more lost value, house foreclosures and underwater mortgages than anywhere in the world, as we note in Chapter 4. Recovery has been slow and painful, even five years after the crash.

The problems run even deeper than recession indicators or government budget deficits, however. While California has a long history as a financial center and a place of periodic financial shenanigans, as discussed in Chapter 3, it has been Wall Street West when it comes to the present age of greed, going back to Michael Milken's dodgy Junk Bond empire run out of LA and the Savings and Loan debacle of the 1980s. In the 2000s, California banks such as Countrywide Savings and Golden West Savings were the worst offenders in issuing subprime, adjustable rate, and jumbo mortgages, setting up homeowners for the fall. And the reason there were so many people ready to take the bait was that house prices had bloated up out of reach of ordinary household incomes, which had been stagnant for years among the lower half of wage earners, as noted in Chapter 4.

Even more disturbing in light of California's history of relative equality and a wide middle class, the state has recently been in the vanguard when it comes to widening inequality. On the one hand, wages and salaries have gone nowhere fast, and poverty rates have shot up with every recession, as remarked upon in Chapters 3 and 8. On the other hand, people at the top have done all too well. The top 10 to 20 percent of professional, technical, and managerial workers have ridden their skills and position to happy heights on the tsunami of high-tech profits. Even worse has been the untrammeled enrichment of the top 1 percent—even 0.1 percent—of wealth holders. California has more billionaires and millionaires than any other state, led by tech heroes, movie moguls and investment bankers. Companies like Apple, Chevron, and Wells Fargo are awash in money.

At the same time, inequality has grown to the worst levels in US history, California has become the most racially diverse state in the country, in which the vast majority of working people are people of color, and Whites have become a minority. California is one of the great experiments of our time in the potential for a racially blended society, the hope—never realized—of the Great American Melting Pot and the possibility of a non-White working class joining the ranks of that other idolized entity, the Great American Middle Class. There are certainly hopeful signs, such as the rising percentage of mixed-race children in the state and the surging numbers of young college students of color on the campuses of the state colleges and universities. But the obstacles to full admission to the California Dream are considerable. Today's youth are being hit from all directions: by more poverty, greater hunger, worse schools, and grimmer job prospects, as seen in Chapters 7 and 8.

Meanwhile, some of California's greatest material accomplishments of the past have gone sour and left serious problems for today's citizens. The wastelands and toxicity of the mining era are still with us, especially in the Sacramento Valley. Clear cutting of timber and the roads built into the Klamath and Siskiyou mountains have left the North Coast with a legacy of silted and clogged rivers. The industrial farming practiced by California agribusiness has left its mark, with pesticides and nitrates in groundwater, toxic runoff, and saline soils throughout the Central Valley. We detail these problems in Chapter 6, which looks more closely at air and water pollution. There, too, we take up the most salient output of modern California, carbon emissions, and the chilling prospects of climate change.

To their credit, Californians have often been the first to see the damage of unrestricted industrialization and urbanization, and to call for preservation and restoration of the natural landscape. No place has been more aggressive in taking up the cudgels in defense of the

Earth, perhaps because the despoliation of our magnificent natural heritage has been more readily apparent than almost anywhere else. California has been a leader in the conservation movement since the days of John Muir and the founding of the Sierra Club. It led the way in the postwar era, with fights over oil spills and coastal reserves, dams and wild rivers, mountain resorts and wilderness areas, pesticides and farmworker protection, wetlands and bay fill, and much more besides.

Today, California's government has been among the few in the USA to take heed of global warming and to enact policies for energy conservation and carbon controls. Californians are leading the way in solar energy, electric vehicles, green buildings, and other technologies, and in trying to rethink the form of cities and means of transit, from the Smart Growth movement to the Critical Mass cry for bicycle-friendly streets.

In short, it is possible for the people of California to change our current trajectory and to create a better future for this wonderful state. To do this, however, it is vital that today's Californians face up to the shortcomings of the Golden State, putting aside the sunny myths of the California Dream, and weighing past successes against the many wrongs. We hope that this atlas can help awaken and prod the public to demand that state government and the powers-that-be do better. We make no pretense of neutrality; the facts presented here constitute a call to action on many fronts, from increased funding to public education to better control of water pollution.

But wait! Is such advocacy a violation of the honest goals of a California atlas? Is an atlas not a neutral purveyor of facts and geographic orientation? Such is the prevalent fiction, but, as the history of geography shows, it is far from true. Of course, atlases are meant to inform, and they should do this in a manner as honest, elegant, and truthful as possible. Nevertheless, maps are a language like any other, in which the speakers pick and choose what they want to say, or what they want the reader to hear. The maps of the Southern California Automobile Association always feature freeways, the hard lines of orientation for Angelinos, but that is only one way of seeing Greater Los Angeles or Southern California. The vegetation map in Chapter 1 looks quite strange by comparison, until one gets used to it; soon the familiar patterns emerge that Southern Californians know well, if they have kept their eyes open. Other maps here may show unknown territory, such as prisons, inequality, or racial segregation, which we hope to make Californians more familiar with. So, dear readers, enter this atlas with eyes wide open, and see what wonderful things—and disorienting ones—await.

Richard A. Walker
Berkeley, May 2013

Suresh K. Lodha
Santa Cruz, May 2013

ACKNOWLEDGMENTS

The authors wish to thank the team at Myriad Editions for their yeo(wo)man work: Jannet King for steering the project skillfully through a deluge of drafts, comments, and changes, and Isabelle Lewis for transforming the data into elegant and creative graphics. Both were incredibly fast, efficient, and full of useful ideas that made this atlas a better finished product. Thanks to Candida Lacey at Myriad and Kim Robinson at UC Press for believing in the project and putting together the whole team.

We thank Nichole Zlatunich, and Hiroshi Fukurai and his students for their early contributions; Ben Crow, Ruth Langridge, Ellen Hanak, and Nico Secunda for their feedback on specific topics; Sandra Taylor and Josh Begley for their contributions on photographs; and two anonymous reviewers for their helpful suggestions.

The following people provided background research on specific topics:

Daniel DeSanto	Hunger & Homelessness
Riley Doyle Evans	Crime & Incarceration
Anthony Hendrix	Water Supply, Water Use
Madhu Lodha	Pre-K Education
Cory Lee Mann	Crime & Incarceration
Molly Solomon	Agriculture
Erin Stephens	Energy Supply, Energy Use, Renewable Energy
Brooke Velasquez	K–12 Education

Richard Walker wishes to thank Annie for her boundless enthusiasm for life and for her tolerance of the time spent bent over his computer. He dedicates this atlas to his favorite Californian, Zia.

Suresh Lodha wishes to thank Madhu for her unwavering care and support. He shares the joy of this atlas with Chandan and Anand.

PHOTO CREDITS

Chapter One

LAND & PEOPLE

California enjoys the most distinctive and varied landscape in North America. It boasts high peaks and sunken valleys, live volcanoes and earthquake faults, rolling hills and lava beds, white water and level plains. Its climate is even rarer, falling between rainy northwest and arid southwest, with a Mediterranean balancing act in between. Coastal fog and alpine snow frame the scene. But nothing prepares the visitor for the astounding array of microclimates and regions, nor for the fantastic biodiversity nestled into the innumerable corners of the state.

California's unique landscape is the stage on which its rich history has played out, leading to claims of three, four or a dozen different Californias divided by mountain ranges, ocean vistas, and water politics. Without a doubt, the wealth of nature has benefitted Californians economically, but it has equally touched their hearts, making this the world center of environmentalism for over a century.

Millions of people have been drawn to California since the Gold Rush, creating a state of permanent migration, both domestic and international. It remains an unsettled place in many ways, a mixing pot that never quite melds. Yet it has been a continual source of wonderment for the diversity of its people and the way they have carved out a way of life—and degree of tolerance and optimism—at odds with so much of the world. Not to be forgotten, however, is the dark side of this collision of peoples from many continents: a dissonant history of racism, repression, and annihilation of the native people.

The lure of California has had many names: the California Dream, the Golden State, the Land of Sunshine. No doubt a favorable climate and hopes for the future have led people to our shores, but the foundations of the state's allure are mostly practical: a thriving economy, lots of jobs, an open society, reuniting families torn asunder, and more. Once here, it is the people, their wits and their labor, who have built the California dreamworks. Few, however, wish to remember the failures and defeats, or simply the bent backs and unrewarded drudgery that mar the gilded image.

California stands at a threshold today. The golden economy has lost some of its luster, inequality is growing, and the state is finding it hard to provide for the new Californians of this generation, the new majority of people of color. What we and they choose to do about it will tell if the Dream stays alive.

Immigrants protesting
against US Congress
Immigration Reform Proposal,
Los Angeles, May 1, 2006.

Land & Nature

California's geography sets it apart from the rest of North America. Its natural blessings have been a source of wonder and wealth, its frequent earthquakes a challenge.

California is so distinct in topography, climate and ecology that it has been called "an island in the land". Facing the Pacific Ocean on the west, it is walled off by high mountains in the north and east and by deserts in the south and southeast. Within that realm lie nine major topographic regions.

Dominating the state's midsection are three parallel regions: Coast Ranges, Central Valley, and Sierra Nevada. Southern California has three regions, as well: Coastal Plain, Transverse Ranges, and Mojave Desert. The Transverse Ranges run east–west, cutting across the grain of the Sierras and Coast Ranges. Northern California has two subregions: Klamath and Siskiyou Mountains on the west and the volcanic landscape of the Southern Cascades to the east. Beyond the Sierra, California shares a piece of Nevada's Basin and Range.

California's landscape is a creation of the tectonics generated by the collision of the Pacific and North American plates. In the distant past, the Pacific floor dove under the continent, pushing up the Sierra (as in today's Cascades). Now the Pacific plate slides along the San Andreas fault system, twisting northwest and pushing upward, creating the Coast and Transverse Ranges, and periodically shaking up California's cities. California has benefited greatly from the gifts of the land: gold, silver, and other minerals left by volcanism and uplift; oil deposits from sea beds driven far beneath the coast; and deep valley soils deposited from ancient mountains.

SISKIYOU MTNS
KLAMATH MTNS
SOUTHERN CASCADES
NORTHERN COAST RANGES
CENTRAL VALLEY
SIERRA NEVADA

1980
1992
1923
2010

San **Andreas** **Fault**

San Francisco • 1868
PACIFIC OCEAN
1838
San Juan Bautista
1906
San Gregorio - Hozri Fault Zone
SOUTHERN COAST RANGES
Parkfield •
1952
1857

Owens Valley Fault
1872
Death Valley
BASIN AND RANGE
Garlock Fault
MOJAVE DESERT
1999
TRANSVERSE RANGES
Los Angeles • 1992
COASTAL PLAIN
Banning Fault
San Jacinto Fault
1940

SAN ANDREAS FAULT SYSTEM
—— fault line
—— fault zone
Segments on which slip occurred during:
—— great earthquakes of 1857, 1872, 1906
—— smaller earthquakes
1857 dates of earthquakes of magnitudes 7 to 8

EARTHQUAKES
Over magnitude 6.0
1906–2012

Bar chart labels: San Francisco, offshore Cape Mendocino, Lompoc, Imperial Valley, Kern County, offshore Humboldt County, Cape Mendocino, Landers, Hector Mine, El Mayor-Cucapah

Y-axis: 8.0, 7.5, 7.0, 6.5, 6.0

X-axis: 1906, '15, '18, '22 '23 '25 '26 '27, '32 '33 '34, '40 '42, '46 '47 '48, '52, '54, '66, '68 '71, '79 '80, '83 '84 '86 '87 '89, '92 '94, '99, 2003 '04 '05, '10, '12

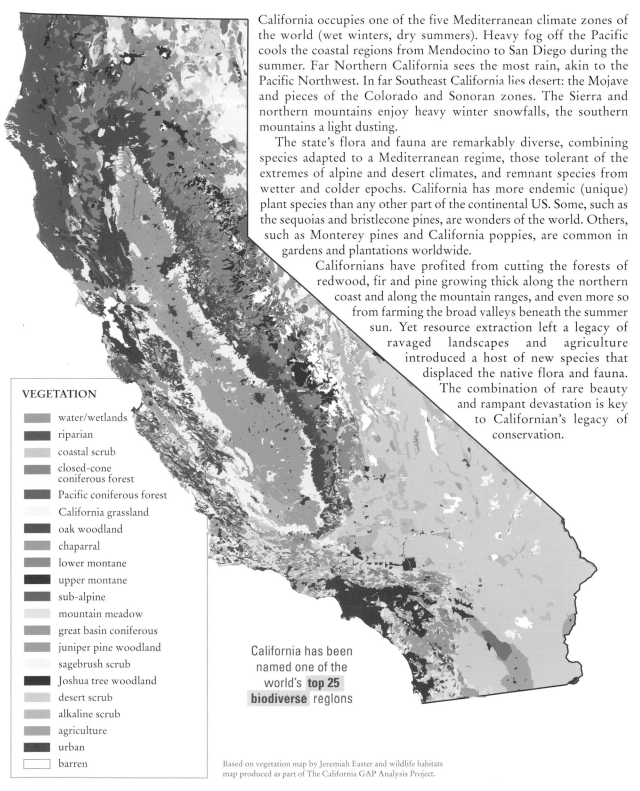

California occupies one of the five Mediterranean climate zones of the world (wet winters, dry summers). Heavy fog off the Pacific cools the coastal regions from Mendocino to San Diego during the summer. Far Northern California sees the most rain, akin to the Pacific Northwest. In far Southeast California lies desert: the Mojave and pieces of the Colorado and Sonoran zones. The Sierra and northern mountains enjoy heavy winter snowfalls, the southern mountains a light dusting.

The state's flora and fauna are remarkably diverse, combining species adapted to a Mediterranean regime, those tolerant of the extremes of alpine and desert climates, and remnant species from wetter and colder epochs. California has more endemic (unique) plant species than any other part of the continental US. Some, such as the sequoias and bristlecone pines, are wonders of the world. Others, such as Monterey pines and California poppies, are common in gardens and plantations worldwide.

Californians have profited from cutting the forests of redwood, fir and pine growing thick along the northern coast and along the mountain ranges, and even more so from farming the broad valleys beneath the summer sun. Yet resource extraction left a legacy of ravaged landscapes and agriculture introduced a host of new species that displaced the native flora and fauna. The combination of rare beauty and rampant devastation is key to Californian's legacy of conservation.

VEGETATION

- water/wetlands
- riparian
- coastal scrub
- closed-cone coniferous forest
- Pacific coniferous forest
- California grassland
- oak woodland
- chaparral
- lower montane
- upper montane
- sub-alpine
- mountain meadow
- great basin coniferous
- juniper pine woodland
- sagebrush scrub
- Joshua tree woodland
- desert scrub
- alkaline scrub
- agriculture
- urban
- barren

California has been named one of the world's **top 25 biodiverse** regions

Based on vegetation map by Jeremiah Easter and wildlife habitats map produced as part of The California GAP Analysis Project.

19

PUBLIC LANDS & PARKS

Half of California's land is in public ownership, and much of that is protected in the most extensive system of national, state, and local parks in the United States.

⋯⋯⋯⋯⋯⋯⋯⋯⋯⋯⋯⋯⋯⋯⋯⋯⋯⋯

FOUNDING OF CALIFORNIA'S STATE PARKS
Number established in each five-year period
1889–2010

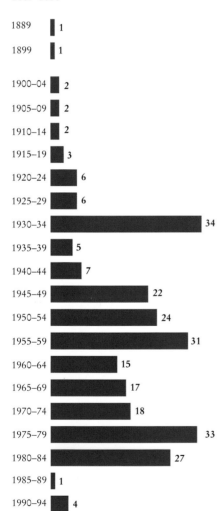

Period	Number
1889	1
1899	1
1900–04	2
1905–09	2
1910–14	2
1915–19	3
1920–24	6
1925–29	6
1930–34	34
1935–39	5
1940–44	7
1945–49	22
1950–54	24
1955–59	31
1960–64	15
1965–69	17
1970–74	18
1975–79	33
1980–84	27
1985–89	1
1990–94	4
1995–99	4
2000–04	11
2005–09	2

Large areas of California are in public ownership, mostly federal lands administered by the US Forest Service, National Park Service and Bureau of Land Management. Public lands occupy over 47 million acres—almost half of the state's 100 million acres. Only Alaska and Nevada have more acreage in public lands.

California has more units of the National Parks system (monuments, historic sites, seashores, reserves, recreation areas) than any other state (32), covering 7.5 million acres. Yosemite and Sequoia were two of the earliest national parks, and Yosemite Valley is arguably the oldest in the country (given to the state to administer in 1864). The National Park Service (1916) was the brainchild of Stephen Mather, the first of several Californians to serve as its director.

National forests began to be set aside in 1884 after most of the west had been sold into private hands. Almost 2 million acres of redwood forests were disposed of before the country woke up to the devastation of uncontrolled logging. California now has the second highest national forest area of any state: 20.7 million acres. Californians led the fight for the National Wilderness Preservation System (1964) and the state has more wilderness areas than any other, lying mostly in national forests. Desert lands were long thought of as useless, except for military purposes, but large tracts have recently been set aside in parks, such as the Mojave National Preserve.

California has the largest state park system in the country: 278 units encompassing 1.4 million acres, including parks, historic sites, natural reserves, and recreation areas. Most are smaller than national parks, but they attract almost twice the number of visitors. The first historic site was marked in 1889 and the first park created in 1902, but a state parks system was not organized and financed until 1928, growing rapidly thereafter. Today, the state's perennial budget crisis has hit the parks hard, with few new units added and many closed to regular use.

California's urban areas are packed with city, county and regional parks and open spaces, adding up to more than 1.5 million acres. Offshore, the state has thousands of square miles covered by four federal marine sanctuaries. The state has also designated over 100 state marine protected areas, and development along the 1,000-mile coastline has been tightly regulated since 1972. San Francisco Bay has been protected from further incursions since 1965 and includes five of the over 50 national wildlife refuges in the state.

Californians have been leaders in national and global conservation for over a century. The movement has been inspired by the state's magnificent landscape and by the devastation of the land by mining, logging, and urbanization. Since the days of John Muir, its momentum has never slowed, taking on new threats to the land and waters as they arose, such as large dams, ski resorts, suburban sprawl, bay fill, and coastal development. Today's conservationists focus on climate change, energy conservation, and rethinking cities.

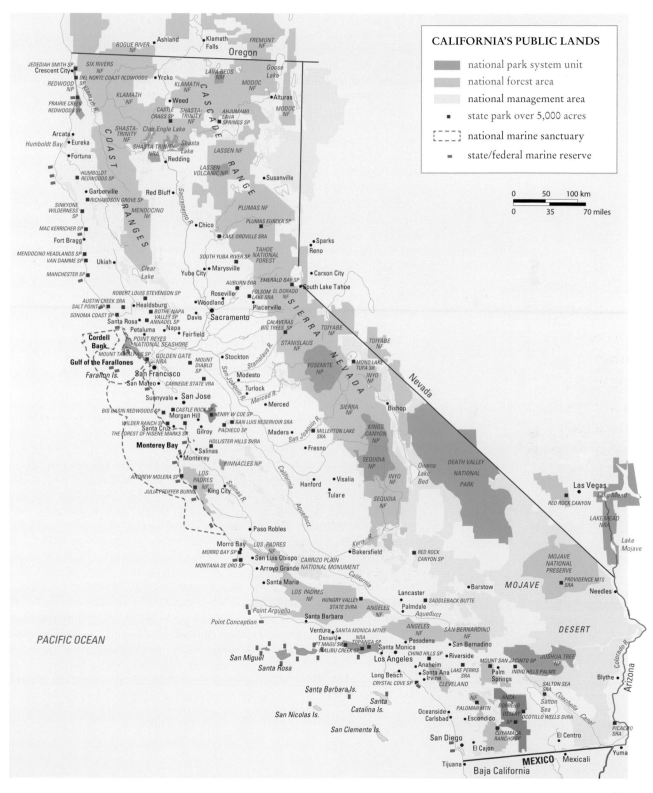

COLONIALISM & NATIVE CALIFORNIANS

California was part of the Spanish Empire, then Mexico, before being annexed to the United States. Native peoples were annihilated by Spaniards, Mexicans, and Americans alike, through forced removal, slave labor, disease and massacres, and are still struggling to regain their rightful place in state life.

Native Californians arrived more than 10,000 years ago. They lived in families and clans of exceptional diversity, speaking 100 languages and 300 dialects. They prospered on the abundant wildlife, which they managed through seed collection, land-clearing fires, and fish ponds. Their numbers reached perhaps 300,000 in pre-Colonial times, the largest concentration north of the Valley of Mexico, but unlike the Iroquois they did not form nations.

The Spaniards reached California in 1542, but left it alone until their empire was threatened in the late 18th century by British, French, Russian, and American expansion. The Christianizing Missions founded by Father Junipero Serra, where natives were forced to live and work, brought devastation through disease and destruction of past ways of life. Native numbers fell by one-third to one-half, especially along the coast.

The Mexican era after 1821 brought new trials to people further inland and northward. Mexican rancheros exploited the natives as indentured labor, while building a trade in hides and tallow. Again, thousands of the natives perished. The Mexican–American war in 1844–46 brought California under the sway of the US, which annexed the northern half of Mexico in 1848.

Following this, the Gold Rush drew in some 300,000 fortune seekers. Miners overran the last mountain redoubts of the native peoples, and many were enslaved. Nowhere were American Indians treated worse. The first governor, Peter Burnett, called for the extermination of native tribes, a task aided and abetted by state militias. California opposed Indian Reservations and federal agents were notoriously corrupt, leaving most native people landless and scattered. There are over 100 recognized tribes in California, but most bands never reclaimed lands other than tiny rancherias.

The population of Native Americans fell to a low of 15,000 by 1900, then started a slow recovery, often through mixing with the conquering people. Estimates depend on the criteria for inclusion, but have increased rapidly since 1950. Before that, many did not want to identify as a disparaged people; but with the rebellions of the 1960s native heritage became a source of pride, swelling the census count. In addition, Native Californians migrated to the cities, where they were joined by tens of thousands of American Indians from around the west, forced from reservations by poverty and the federal decertification of tribes. By 1970 they were outnumbered by new migrants, and numbers were climbing fast. The urbanization and mixing of tribes gave rise to the American Indian Movement, ignited when young militants seized Alcatraz in 1969 and proclaimed it liberated territory. Today, there is a renewed pride in learning native languages, crafts, and culture.

The legalization of native-run casinos, over 60 in 2011, has earned more than $7 billion. The income has been used to improve housing, restore tribal lands, and improve education, but has led to disputes over tribal membership. After 200 years of oppression, Native Americans are still struggling to preserve their identities and culture and finding it an uphill task to attain the same level of education, health, and liberties as other minorities do.

CALIFORNIA EMERGING FROM MEXICO
1848–53

- area ceded by Mexico to USA in Treaty of Guadalupe Hidalgo (1848)
- area sold by Mexico to USA in Gadsden Purchase (1853)
- present-day Mexico
- - - - present-day US state boundaries
- ——— present-day Mexico–USA border

USA

Texas
(1836–1845)

MEXICO

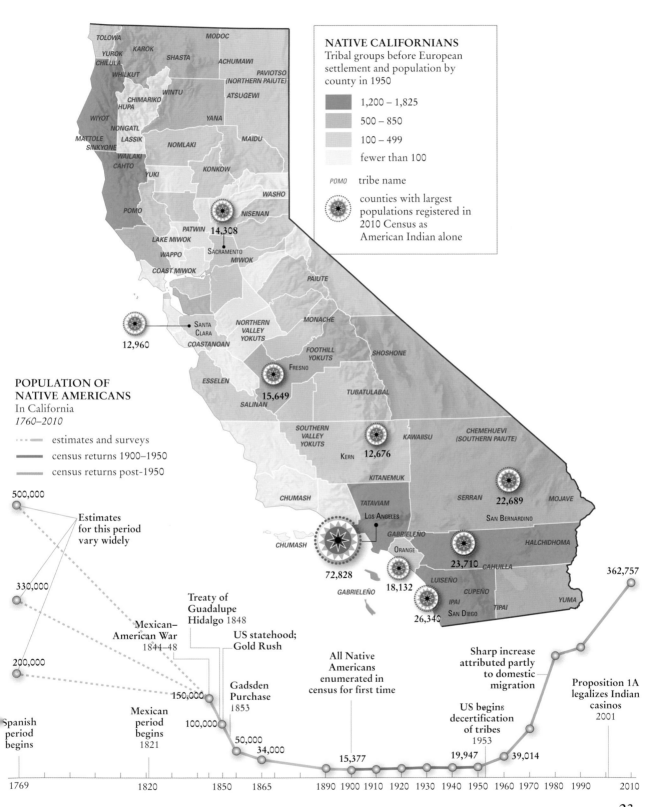

NATIVE CALIFORNIANS

Tribal groups before European settlement and population by county in 1950

- 1,200 – 1,825
- 500 – 850
- 100 – 499
- fewer than 100

POMO tribe name

counties with largest populations registered in 2010 Census as American Indian alone

TOLOWA
KAROK
MODOC
YUROK
SHASTA
CHILULA
ACHUMAWI
WHILKUT
PAVIOTSO (NORTHERN PAIUTE)
CHIMARIKO
WINTU
HUPA
ATSUGEWI
WIYOT
YANA
NONGATL
MATTOLE
LASSIK
NOMLAKI
MAIDU
SINKYONE
WAILAKI
CAHTO
KONKOW
YUKI
WASHO
POMO
NISENAN
14,308
PATWIN
SACRAMENTO
LAKE MIWOK
WAPPO
MIWOK
COAST MIWOK
PAIUTE
SANTA CLARA
12,960
NORTHERN VALLEY YOKUTS
MONACHE
COASTANOAN
ESSELEN
FOOTHILL YOKUTS
SHOSHONE
FRESNO
15,649
SALINAN
TUBATULABAL
SOUTHERN VALLEY YOKUTS
CHEMEHUEVI (SOUTHERN PAIUTE)
KERN
12,676
KAWAIISU
KITANEMUK
CHUMASH
TATAVIAM
SERRAN
MOJAVE
LOS ANGELES
22,689
SAN BERNARDINO
CHUMASH
GABRIELEÑO
72,828
ORANGE
HALCHIDHOMA
GABRIELEÑO
18,132
23,710
CAHUILLA
LUISEÑO
CUPEÑO
IPAI
YUMA
SAN DIEGO
TIPAI
26,340

POPULATION OF NATIVE AMERICANS

In California
1760–2010

- · · · · estimates and surveys
- ——— census returns 1900–1950
- ——— census returns post-1950

500,000

Estimates for this period vary widely

330,000

200,000

Spanish period begins

Mexican period begins 1821

Mexican–American War 1844–48

Treaty of Guadalupe Hidalgo 1848

US statehood; Gold Rush

Gadsden Purchase 1853

150,000

100,000

50,000

34,000

All Native Americans enumerated in census for first time

15,377

US begins decertification of tribes 1953

19,947

Sharp increase attributed partly to domestic migration

39,014

Proposition 1A legalizes Indian casinos 2001

362,757

1769   1820   1850   1865   1890 1900 1910 1920 1930 1940 1950 1960 1970 1980 1990   2010

23

POPULATION

California is the most populous state in the United States and for decades was among the fastest growing, due to high immigration and birth rates.

RACE/ETHNICITY AND ORIGIN
2010

- White
- White Hispanic or Latino
- non-White Hispanic or Latino
- Black or African American
- American Indian and Alaska alone
- Asian
- Native Hawaiian and other Pacific Islander alone
- some other race
- two or more races

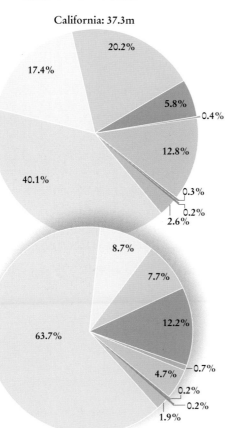

California: 37.3m

20.2%
17.4%
5.8%
0.4%
12.8%
0.3%
0.2%
2.6%
40.1%

8.7%
7.7%
12.2%
63.7%
0.7%
4.7%
0.2%
0.2%
1.9%

USA: 308.7m

Nearly one-eighth of people in the United States live in California; no other state is close. California has long boasted rapid population growth, drawing in large numbers of migrants from other countries and from elsewhere in the USA, because of its continuous economic expansion and demand for labor. The weakened economy slowed the increase in the 2000s, making it the decade of least growth since the Gold Rush and the first when more people were born in California than moved into it. Immigration was way down from its peak in the 1980s, and there was no net migration from other states. Even so, California's population rose from 34 million to 37 million between 2000 and 2010, and should exceed 40 million by 2020.

Currently, 27 percent of California's people are foreign-born, compared to 13 percent for the United States as a whole. Hispanics/Latinos made up more than a third of California's population in 2010 and will soon pass Euro-Americans/Whites, whose share has fallen from over 90 percent in 1960 to 40 percent today. Asians overtook African-Americans as the next largest category in the 1980s. Native Americans make up fewer than 1 percent of the state's population. Mixed race, at 2.6 percent, is an undercounted but growing category.

The age distribution is that of a mature economy, with a large number of baby boomers retiring in the next 20 years. But the age distribution of immigrants is younger than that of the American-born, and they have larger families, on average. This key group provides the bulk of the labor force today and will continue to do so in the near future.

Although most people are concentrated in the coastal metropolitan areas of Los Angeles, the Bay Area, and San Diego, rapid growth is occurring in the Inland Empire of Riverside and San Bernardino counties in Southern California, and the Central Valley from Sacramento to Bakersfield in Northern California. The geographic distribution of people by ethnicity/race and national origin is also uneven: Whites dominate in the mountainous areas, while Hispanics/Latinos are disproportionate in the inland valleys. The coastal cities are the most mixed.

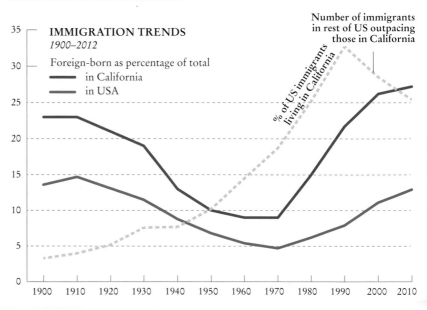

IMMIGRATION TRENDS
1900–2012

Foreign-born as percentage of total
— in California
— in USA

% of US immigrants living in California

Number of immigrants in rest of US outpacing those in California

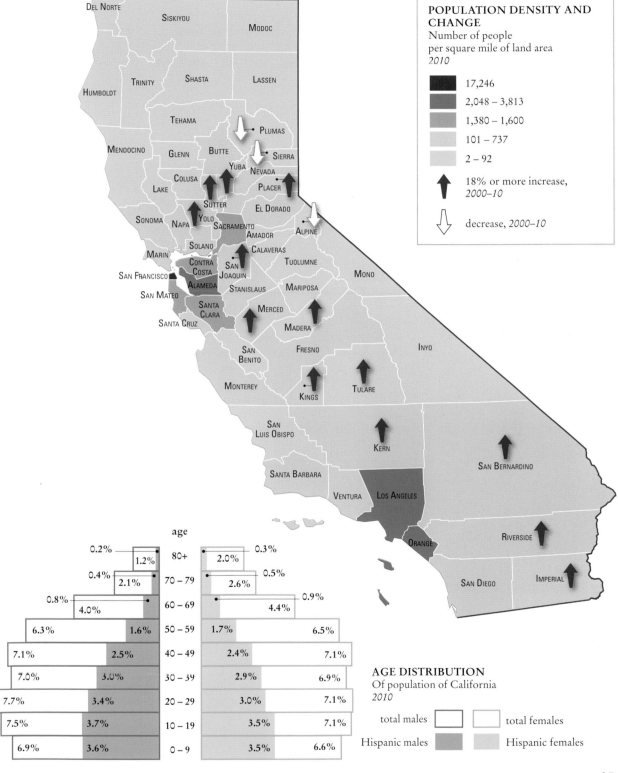

POPULATION DENSITY AND CHANGE
Number of people
per square mile of land area
2010

■	17,246
■	2,048 – 3,813
■	1,380 – 1,600
□	101 – 737
□	2 – 92

↑ 18% or more increase, 2000–10

⇩ decrease, 2000–10

Del Norte · Siskiyou · Modoc · Trinity · Shasta · Lassen · Humboldt · Tehama · Mendocino · Butte · Plumas · Glenn · Sierra · Colusa · Yuba · Nevada · Lake · Sutter · Placer · El Dorado · Sonoma · Yolo · Napa · Sacramento · Amador · Alpine · Marin · Solano · Calaveras · San Francisco · Contra Costa · San Joaquin · Tuolumne · San Mateo · Alameda · Stanislaus · Mono · Santa Clara · Mariposa · Santa Cruz · Merced · Madera · San Benito · Fresno · Inyo · Monterey · Kings · Tulare · San Luis Obispo · Kern · San Bernardino · Santa Barbara · Los Angeles · Ventura · Orange · Riverside · San Diego · Imperial

AGE DISTRIBUTION
Of population of California
2010

total males □ — □ total females
Hispanic males ■ — ■ Hispanic females

age

0.2% / 1.2%	80+	2.0% / 0.3%
0.4% / 2.1%	70 – 79	2.6% / 0.5%
0.8% / 4.0%	60 – 69	4.4% / 0.9%
6.3% / 1.6%	50 – 59	1.7% / 6.5%
7.1% / 2.5%	40 – 49	2.4% / 7.1%
7.0% / 3.0%	30 – 39	2.9% / 6.9%
7.7% / 3.4%	20 – 29	3.0% / 7.1%
7.5% / 3.7%	10 – 19	3.5% / 7.1%
6.9% / 3.6%	0 – 9	3.5% / 6.6%

25

MIGRATION

For centuries, California has been a magnet for migrants, both domestic and foreign. They have come from many places in search of a better life, escaping poverty, war, famine, and persecution—but often facing hostility on arrival.

Yearning for a better life, domestic and foreign migrants have poured into California throughout its history. They have come to search for gold, work as laborers, establish businesses, unify families, and escape poverty and persecution. They have been attracted to California for its jobs, openness, climate, and opportunities to realize one's dreams.

In 1848 the cry of gold drew fortune-seekers from the East Coast, Europe, Latin America, and China. Chinese and Irish came as laborers to build the transcontinental railroad and to work in agriculture and manufacturing. Germans, Scots, and Scandinavians came as skilled workers. By the 1900s, farmers were drawing on new sources from Japan, the Philippines, and India.

During this period, California suffered serious outbreaks of anti-immigrant agitation: anti-Chinese in the 1870s, anti-Japanese in the 1900s, and anti-Mexican in the 1920s. These eruptions influenced national policies, such as the ban against Chinese entry in 1882, the restriction of Japanese immigration after 1908, and forced sterilization in the 1920s. Californians helped pass the Quota and Immigration Acts of 1921 and 1924 that resulted in a dramatic drop in immigration for the next 50 years.

The explosive growth of Los Angeles from 1900 to 1930 lured millions of White Americans west, as well as tens of thousands of Mexicans and African-Americans. The Dust Bowl of the 1930s drove thousands of poor Whites, popularly known as "Okies", to California, who moved to the cities in World War II along with large numbers of new migrants, White and Black, from the south.

The postwar boom drew millions more domestic migrants, but when domestic sources ran dry immigrants took their place. From 1942 to 1964, the "temporary" Bracero Program brought more than 4 million agricultural workers from Mexico into California. Then, with the lifting of quotas in 1965, millions of Mexicans, Central Americans, and many nationalities from Asia joined the rush to California.

AGE PROFILE
Percentage of foreign-born population in each age bracket
2011

Median age: 43.8 years

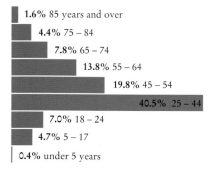

- **1.6%** 85 years and over
- **4.4%** 75 – 84
- **7.8%** 65 – 74
- **13.8%** 55 – 64
- **19.8%** 45 – 54
- **40.5%** 25 – 44
- **7.0%** 18 – 24
- **4.7%** 5 – 17
- **0.4%** under 5 years

HISTORICAL GROWTH
Foreign-born immigrants in California as percentage of population *1850–2010*

1882 date of Federal actions

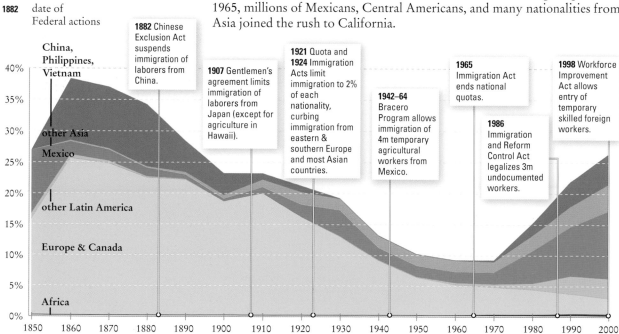

1882 Chinese Exclusion Act suspends immigration of laborers from China.

1907 Gentlemen's agreement limits immigration of laborers from Japan (except for agriculture in Hawaii).

1921 Quota and **1924** Immigration Acts limit immigration to 2% of each nationality, curbing immigration from eastern & southern Europe and most Asian countries.

1942–64 Bracero Program allows immigration of 4m temporary agricultural workers from Mexico.

1965 Immigration Act ends national quotas.

1986 Immigration and Reform Control Act legalizes 3m undocumented workers.

1998 Workforce Improvement Act allows entry of temporary skilled foreign workers.

China, Philippines, Vietnam

other Asia

Mexico

other Latin America

Europe & Canada

Africa

California has welcomed many political refugees over the years, including European émigrés after the revolutions of 1848, Filipinos uprooted by the American takeover of 1899, and "boat people" escaping Vietnam after 1975. But some of the worst anti-immigrant reactions came with the internment of Japanese in 1942, mass deportation of Mexicans in 1954 to 1955, and the infamous border wall with Mexico in the 1990s.

Although California continues to be the nation's most immigrant-rich state, the rate of growth of the immigrant population, which peaked in the 1980s, is now one of the slowest in the nation. Several new immigrant gateways have emerged, dispersing the immigrant population much more widely across the United States.

CALIFORNIA'S IMMIGRANT POPULATION
By country of origin
2011

Total: 10.2m

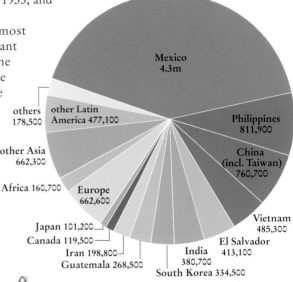

- Mexico 4.3m
- Philippines 811,900
- China (incl. Taiwan) 760,700
- Vietnam 485,300
- El Salvador 413,100
- India 380,700
- South Korea 334,500
- Guatemala 268,500
- Iran 198,800
- Canada 119,500
- Japan 101,200
- Africa 160,700
- Europe 662,600
- other Asia 662,300
- other Latin America 477,100
- others 178,500

FOREIGN-BORN POPULATION
As percentage of population
2011

- 20% or more
- 10% – 19.9%
- 5% – 9.9%
- less than 5%

Percentage growth in foreign-born population, *2000–11*
- 75% or more
- 25% or less

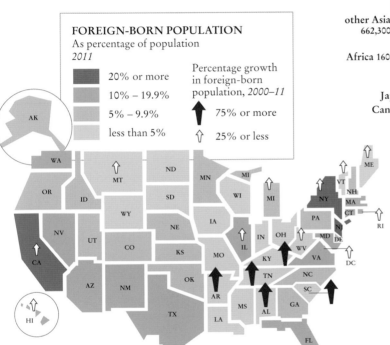

EDUCATIONAL CHARACTERISTICS
2011

US-born population   foreign-born population

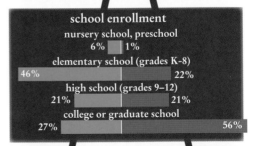

school enrollment

nursery school, preschool
6%   1%

elementary school (grades K-8)
46%   22%

high school (grades 9–12)
21%   21%

college or graduate school
27%   56%

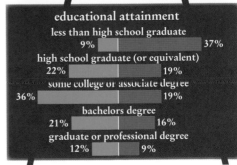

educational attainment

less than high school graduate
9%   37%

high school graduate (or equivalent)
22%   19%

some college or associate degree
36%   19%

bachelors degree
21%   16%

graduate or professional degree
12%   9%

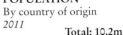

ECONOMIC CHARACTERISTICS
2011

US-born population   foreign-born population

median age
29.5   43.8

in labor force
62.2%   65.9%

median income (men)
$56,634 $36,294

median income (women)
$45,996 $33,462

27

UNAUTHORIZED IMMIGRATION

California has the highest number of unauthorized immigrants of any state. Although their presence is controversial, several industries depend on them to fill low-wage, low-skill jobs.

California has the most unauthorized immigrants in the country, about 2.8 million in 2011. The state's share of the country's unauthorized immigrants has dropped steeply from its peak in 1990, and has grown little since 2005 due to the Great Recession and stepped-up federal deportations.

Unauthorized, or undocumented, immigration can either mean crossing the border illegally or overstaying a visa. Most such immigrants are from Mexico, but they include Canadian workers, students from Europe and grandmothers from China. Immigration reform is a hotly contested issue in which California has a major stake; the Immigration Reform Act (1986) regularized over 1 million people in the state. One side considers unauthorized entry to be illegal and such immigrants to be a drain on US resources, calling for stiffer border patrols and deportations. The other side sees unauthorized immigrants as net contributors to the country and wants to see their status legalized with a path to citizenship.

Jobs are the main draw for unauthorized immigrants, and many US employers are eager to hire them because they accept low pay and are unable to protest working conditions. They are employed mostly in low-skilled, manual labor in farming, construction, restaurants, and manufacturing, or as gardeners, janitors, and domestics. Most studies indicate that unauthorized immigrants have little effect on either the employment rates or the wages of US-born workers. Family unification is another major pull for such immigrants.

Most unauthorized immigrants live in poverty, with family incomes half those of US-born citizens. Although some have argued that unauthorized immigrants come for the welfare payments, they remain ineligible for most public-benefit programs. A significant majority of unauthorized immigrants pay income taxes and they contribute billions of dollars to social security which they cannot claim.

California now allows unauthorized immigrants to obtain a driver's license if they arrived before age 16, are under 30, and are enrolled in school or graduated from high school. California's stance is in stark contrast with that of states such as Arizona, which has clamped down on "illegals". The federal government, which has deported millions of unauthorized immigrants in the last few years, is moving toward comprehensive immigration reform that will open up a path to legal residency for unauthorized entrants who would like to become American citizens.

CALIFORNIA'S SHARE
Of unauthorized immigrants to USA
1980–2011

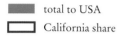

total to USA

California share

32%

1980: 3.1m

42%

1990: 3.6m

29%

2000: 8.5m

24%

2011: 11.5m

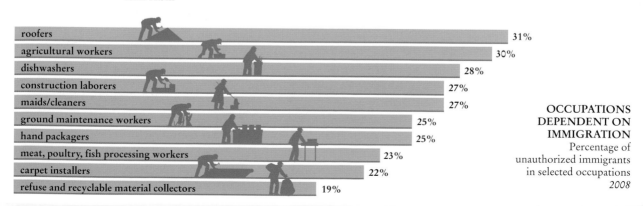

roofers	31%
agricultural workers	30%
dishwashers	28%
construction laborers	27%
maids/cleaners	27%
ground maintenance workers	25%
hand packagers	25%
meat, poultry, fish processing workers	23%
carpet installers	22%
refuse and recyclable material collectors	19%

OCCUPATIONS DEPENDENT ON IMMIGRATION
Percentage of unauthorized immigrants in selected occupations
2008

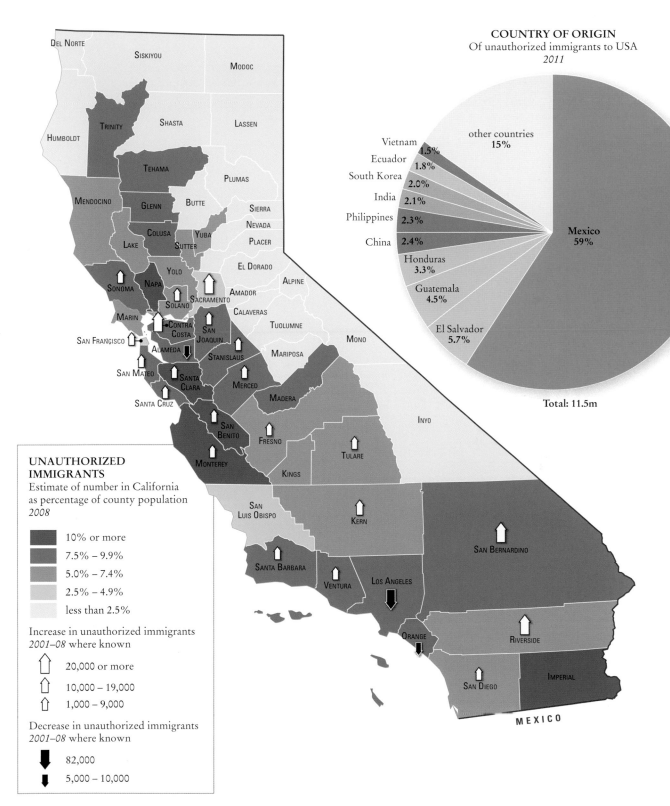

COUNTRY OF ORIGIN
Of unauthorized immigrants to USA
2011

Vietnam 1.5%
Ecuador 1.8%
South Korea 2.0%
India 2.1%
Philippines 2.3%
China 2.4%
Honduras 3.3%
Guatemala 4.5%
El Salvador 5.7%

other countries 15%

Mexico 59%

Total: 11.5m

**UNAUTHORIZED
IMMIGRANTS**
Estimate of number in California
as percentage of county population
2008

- 10% or more
- 7.5% – 9.9%
- 5.0% – 7.4%
- 2.5% – 4.9%
- less than 2.5%

Increase in unauthorized immigrants
2001–08 where known

- 20,000 or more
- 10,000 – 19,000
- 1,000 – 9,000

Decrease in unauthorized immigrants
2001–08 where known

- 82,000
- 5,000 – 10,000

29

Chapter Two

POLITICS, GOVERNANCE, & POWER

Government and politics may seem far away from immediate concerns about economic livelihood or children's welfare, but government is central to the way we organize our common concerns, from education, health, and public safety to decent roads and clean drinking water. Politics is how we make collective decisions about what government ought to do. Both have failed the people of California in recent times.

Government remains elusive to common citizens, given the labyrinth of branches, agencies, and offices. The federal system of national, state, and local governments adds to the difficulty, with responsibilities sometimes divided, other times shared. The powerful federal government seems far away from local concerns, but local governments appear too weak to handle most social needs. State government and politics loom large in any discussion of the present welfare and future of California.

Yet California's state government has often stumbled in carrying out its obligations. The legislature has been hamstrung because of supermajority requirements, term limits, loss of staff, and the power of lobbyists. Governors have come and gone without giving the state a clear direction. And the numerous confounding propositions on every ballot limit the flexibility of legislators and governors. Meanwhile, the power of money to determine political outcomes has only increased with greater inequality and weaker limitations on political contributions.

A major stumbling block to effective government in California has been budgetary woes. Fiscal crises loom with every economic downturn, thanks chiefly to revenue limits installed by those who wished to lower taxes and shrink spending. California has paid a steep price in damage to collective goals, such as good schools, healthcare for the aged, and a well-trained work force.

A major function of the federal government is the military, which has had a huge impact on the landscape and economy of California. Its looming presence affects politics, as well, as in San Diego's large conservative bloc of former military personnel. Another key function, responsibility for criminal law and prisons, is chiefly lodged at the state level. California mounted a fierce offensive against crime that drew millions of citizens—mostly young, male, Black or Latino—into the justice system and sent far too many to prison. The state's massive buildup of prisons has cut into other government priorities.

Despite California's liberal reputation, it has been a leader in conservative movements for law and order, tax cutting and greater military power for many years. In recent elections, however, it has swung back the other way, and the influence of a new generation of Californians may take it much further in a progressive direction.

Tehachapi Prison, Kern County.

GOVERNMENT & POLITICS

Democracy in California has long suffered from unequal representation, a weak party system, and the power of money in elections. But voting patterns are solidly Democratic and have become more so in recent elections.

California's representative democracy has been diminished by a reduced electorate, supermajority requirements, and the influence of money. Of the state's adult population, only 85 percent are eligible to vote because of the exclusion of immigrants (non-citizens and unauthorized) and the incarcerated. Of those, fewer than three-fourths register and fewer than half go to the polls. Among Latinos and Asians, the proportions are even smaller. Hence, the electorate in California is disproportionately White, as well as older and wealthier than the populace.

Party politics are weak in California, with only half of eligible voters declaring a party affiliation. The registered electorate consists of 43 percent Democrats, 30 percent Republicans, and 21 percent independents. While the Democratic Party has dominated the legislature for over 50 years, Republicans have exercised undue power because of supermajority (two-thirds) voting requirements to pass taxes and budgets (the latter ended in 2010). Californians also voted, in 2010, to adopt a system in which the top two candidates in the primaries, regardless of party, advance to the final election.

California is the most prolific user of ballot initiatives. While such propositions are thought of as a means of popular control, signatures and campaigns are overwhelmingly paid for by wealthy interests. The legislature has been diminished by term limits and staff cuts, making lobbyists more powerful than ever. California is the birthplace of modern media-driven campaigns, whose expense—the highest outside of Presidential races—heightens the influence of rich individual and corporate donors.

California's first constitution was written in 1849, a year before the state was admitted to the union. Many of its radical democratic provisions were undone by subsequent racist legislation. A second constitution was drawn up in 1879, after a popular revolt against big business, and has been amended many times. In 1911, the Progressives swept to power and passed major reforms, including the referendum, recall, and initiative. For almost a century after the Civil War, California was solidly Republican and San Francisco was the stronghold of Democratic, labor, and liberal politics.

Southern California was the principal cradle of US neo-conservatism, producing such national leaders as Richard Nixon and Ronald Reagan, and such movements as the war on crime, tax revolt, and ending Affirmative Action. Northern California has been known for its liberal leadership in gay and women's equality, environmental protection and immigrant rights. Today, the liberal–conservative split is east–west rather than north–south. With the emergence of a stronger Latino, Asian, and youth vote since 2008, California is tilting in a more liberal direction.

CALIFORNIA'S VOTERS
2012

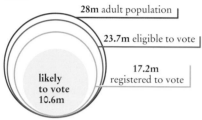

28m adult population
23.7m eligible to vote
17.2m registered to vote
likely to vote 10.6m

RACIAL/ETHNIC BREAKDOWN
2012

- White
- Latino
- Asian
- Black
- other

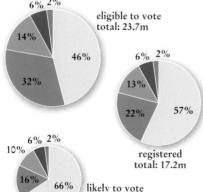

eligible to vote total: 23.7m
6% 2%
14%
32%
46%

registered total: 17.2m
6% 2%
13%
22%
57%

likely to vote total: 10.6m
6% 2%
10%
16%
66%

STATE AND LOCAL GOVERNMENT EMPLOYEES
Number per 10,000 in population and ranking of state in USA
2011 Selected states

10 employees ◯ state ranking

Although California's government is often perceived of as too big, it has one of the lowest rates of government employment.

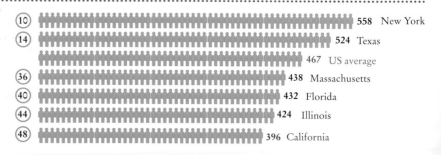

(10)	558 New York
(14)	524 Texas
	467 US average
(36)	438 Massachusetts
(40)	432 Florida
(44)	424 Illinois
(48)	396 California

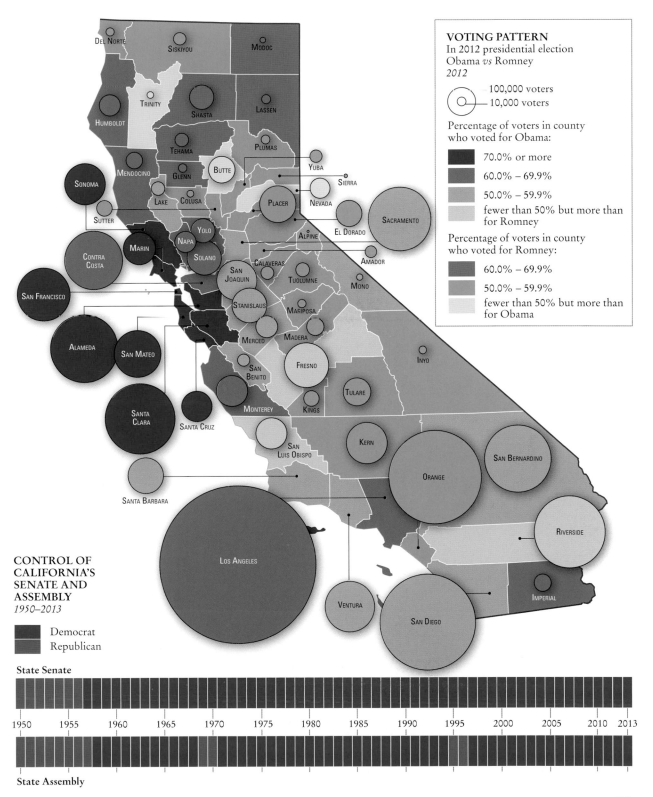

VOTING PATTERN
In 2012 presidential election
Obama *vs* Romney
2012

100,000 voters
10,000 voters

Percentage of voters in county
who voted for Obama:

70.0% or more

60.0% – 69.9%

50.0% – 59.9%

fewer than 50% but more than
for Romney

Percentage of voters in county
who voted for Romney:

60.0% – 69.9%

50.0% – 59.9%

fewer than 50% but more than
for Obama

DEL NORTE
SISKIYOU
MODOC
TRINITY
SHASTA
LASSEN
HUMBOLDT
TEHAMA
PLUMAS
MENDOCINO
GLENN
BUTTE
YUBA
SIERRA
SONOMA
LAKE
COLUSA
PLACER
NEVADA
SUTTER
YOLO
SACRAMENTO
MARIN
NAPA
SOLANO
ALPINE
EL DORADO
CONTRA
COSTA
CALAVERAS
AMADOR
SAN
JOAQUIN
TUOLUMNE
MONO
SAN FRANCISCO
STANISLAUS
ALAMEDA
SAN MATEO
MERCED
MARIPOSA
MADERA
SAN
BENITO
FRESNO
INYO
SANTA
CLARA
SANTA CRUZ
TULARE
MONTEREY
KINGS
SAN
LUIS OBISPO
KERN
SAN BERNARDINO
SANTA BARBARA
ORANGE
RIVERSIDE
LOS ANGELES
IMPERIAL
VENTURA
SAN DIEGO

**CONTROL OF
CALIFORNIA'S
SENATE AND
ASSEMBLY**
1950–2013

Democrat
Republican

State Senate

1950 1955 1960 1965 1970 1975 1980 1985 1990 1995 2000 2005 2010 2013

State Assembly

BUDGET & TAXATION

California has the largest budget after the federal government but has suffered budget shortfalls, revenue volatility, and reduced taxation, resulting in huge cuts during the recession and making planning difficult.

California governments have faced severe fiscal challenges over the last 30 years. This contrasts with robust budget growth in the postwar era, when the state took on greater responsibilities for public education, highways, and social welfare. By 1980, California had the second largest budget after the federal government. Now, every time the economy dips, the state budget goes deeply into the red.

The Great Recession of 2009 to 2012 brought California to its knees. It had the biggest budget deficit of any state, and massive spending cuts forced the furloughing of employees and the issuing of IOUs to employees. The interior counties and cities were the worst affected and, although some local government shortfalls were made up by the state, the cities of Stockton and San Bernardino declared bankruptcy in 2012.

The share of revenue used to pay off the debt on bonds has risen steadily in the last 25 years. Major credit-rating agencies downgraded California's credit in the 2000s, fearful that the state would not be able to keep up with payments to bond holders.

Significant parts of state revenue depend on personal income taxes and sales tax, both of which are tied to economic fluctuations, adding to the volatility of revenues and making planning a challenge.

CALIFORNIA'S DEBT OBLIGATIONS
As percentage of General Fund Expenditures
1990–2013

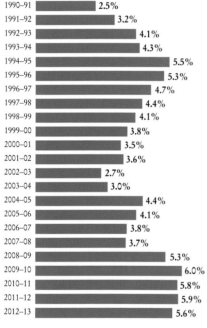

Year	Percentage
1990–91	2.5%
1991–92	3.2%
1992–93	4.1%
1993–94	4.3%
1994–95	5.5%
1995–96	5.3%
1996–97	4.7%
1997–98	4.4%
1998–99	4.1%
1999–00	3.8%
2000–01	3.5%
2001–02	3.6%
2002–03	2.7%
2003–04	3.0%
2004–05	4.4%
2005–06	4.1%
2006–07	3.8%
2007–08	3.7%
2008–09	5.3%
2009–10	6.0%
2010–11	5.8%
2011–12	5.9%
2012–13	5.6%

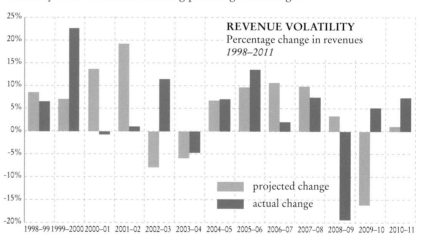

REVENUE VOLATILITY
Percentage change in revenues
1998–2011

- projected change
- actual change

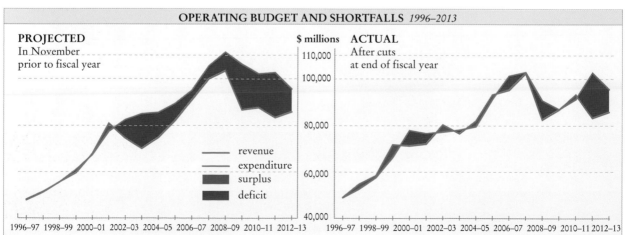

OPERATING BUDGET AND SHORTFALLS *1996–2013*

PROJECTED
In November
prior to fiscal year

$ millions   **ACTUAL**
After cuts
at end of fiscal year

- revenue
- expenditure
- surplus
- deficit

Budgets were regularly deadlocked in the 2000s because the minority Republicans refused all tax increases and the legislature was obliged to pass annual budgets by a two-thirds majority. This practice was ended by Proposition 25 (2010).

State budget deficits are due to a combination of falling revenues in recessions and past tax cuts. Although it is often claimed that taxes are too high, California's tax burden is moderate. With the passage of Proposition 30 in November 2012, Californians voted to levy additional income tax on those making more than $250,000 and an additional 0.25 percent sales tax, increasing state revenue by roughly $6 to $7 billion a year for the next seven years and closing the deficit in 2013.

TAXATION

California is not amongst the top ten states for taxation. Its ratio of taxes to personal income – "tax burden" – has declined by 13 percent since 1977. In 2009, it ranked 11th in terms of combined state and local taxes per person and 16th as a percentage of personal income.

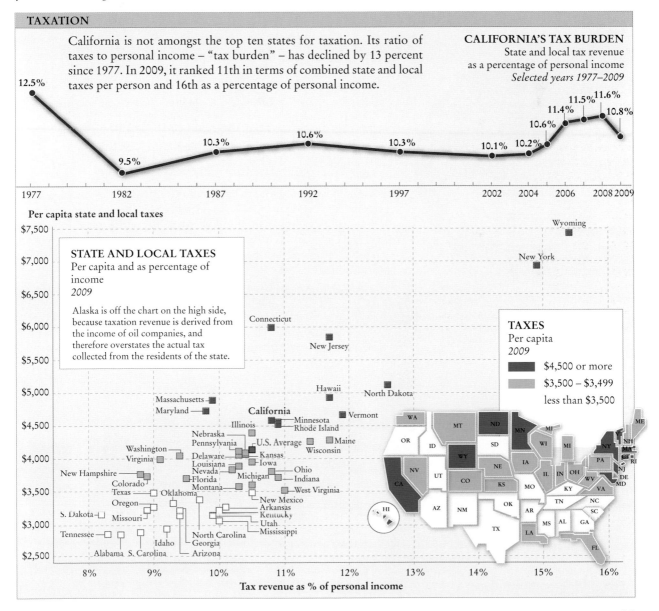

CALIFORNIA'S TAX BURDEN
State and local tax revenue as a percentage of personal income
Selected years 1977–2009

12.5% · 9.5% · 10.3% · 10.6% · 10.3% · 10.1% · 10.2% · 10.6% · 11.4% · 11.5% · 11.6% · 10.8%

1977 · 1982 · 1987 · 1992 · 1997 · 2002 · 2004 · 2006 · 2008 2009

Per capita state and local taxes

STATE AND LOCAL TAXES
Per capita and as percentage of income
2009

Alaska is off the chart on the high side, because taxation revenue is derived from the income of oil companies, and therefore overstates the actual tax collected from the residents of the state.

TAXES
Per capita
2009

$4,500 or more

$3,500 – $3,499

less than $3,500

Tax revenue as % of personal income

GOVERNMENT FINANCES

Tax revenues constitute roughly half of the general revenue of California state and local governments. Two-thirds of expenditure goes to education, health, welfare, and safety.

California state and local governments together are an enterprise worth more than $325 billion. Nearly one-fifth of general revenue comes from the federal government, and the remainder is raised almost equally by the state and local governments. California receives funding from the federal government and, like all states, received higher than normal federal funds between 2009 and 2012 as part of the American Recovery and Reinvestment Act (2009) to combat the Great Recession.

The bulk of the state revenue, roughly $95 billion and referred to as the general budget, comes from taxes on personal income, corporate profits, and retail sales. The state government raises additional revenues of roughly $33 billion using special funds tied to specific expenditure items, such as motor vehicle license fees, and selective sales taxes, as on gasoline, alcohol, and tobacco. Non-tax revenue comes from various charges, including those for higher education, public hospitals, natural resources, and housing.

Local governments once relied on property taxes to raise the bulk of their revenue, but Proposition 13 (1978) reduced these by three-fifths and required a two-thirds vote to approve any new taxes. As a consequence, property taxes now constitute a smaller percentage of total local revenues in comparison to the US average, and California's local governments have had to find other sources of revenue, such as sales and utility taxes, or user fees for such things as parks and garbage collection.

Special districts—by far the most numerous of local governments—provide a way around the financial limits of general governments by imposing taxes and fees tied to their specific functions, such as water supply and flood control. Big cities have long used redevelopment districts to build major projects, using tax increment financing that promised future revenues from rising land values, until they were abolished in 2012.

GENERAL REVENUE
2009–10

☐ raised by taxation

Total Revenue: **$326 billion**

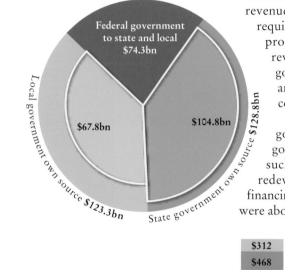

Federal government to state and local $74.3bn

Local government own source $123.3bn

$67.8bn

$104.8bn

State government own source $128.8bn

COMPARISON OF TAX REVENUE SOURCES
California per capita compared with US average and selected states
2009–10

- miscellaneous taxes
- corporation tax
- selective sales taxes*
- sales tax
- income tax
- property tax

* motor fuel, alcohol, tobacco, utility and other selective taxes

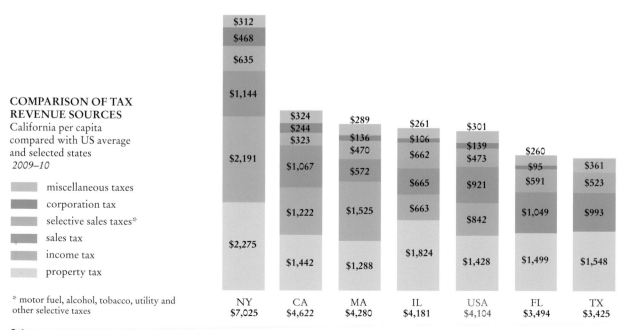

	NY $7,025	CA $4,622	MA $4,280	IL $4,181	USA $4,104	FL $3,494	TX $3,425
miscellaneous	$312	$324	$289	$261	$301	$260	
corporation	$468	$244	$136	$106	$139	$95	$361
selective sales	$635	$323	$470	$662	$473	$591	$523
sales	$1,144	$1,067	$572	$665	$921	$1,049	$993
income	$2,191	$1,222	$1,525	$663	$842		
property	$2,275	$1,442	$1,288	$1,824	$1,428	$1,499	$1,548

36

Education, health, public welfare, and safety are some of the core services provided to the public by state and local government. During the recent recession, the state managed its budget through a combination of cuts to K–12 and higher education, cuts to health programs for children, AIDS patients, domestic violence victims, and Medi-Cal recipients, cuts to social assistance programs by eliminating child-care subsidies and cash assistance for low-income elderly and disabled families, and hefty raises in higher education fees.

In addition to the core services, the government manages more business-like activities in two sectors—public utilities and insurance trusts—with their own sources of revenues and expenditures. Public utilities include water, energy, and transit facilities, sometimes operated by private firms under government oversight. The insurance trust sector includes public retirement systems, as well as social and life insurance programs, such as unemployment compensation, workers compensation, and state medical and disability funds. Insurance trust revenues suffered dramatic losses due to negative investment returns during the recent recession.

California state government has a long-term outstanding debt of $84 billion—equal to about 90 percent of its annual general fund budget. Large outlays for state and local public works, such as school facilities, new roads and light rail, clean water and disaster preparedness, convention centers, and parks, are normally paid for by issuing bonds.

GENERAL EXPENDITURE
State and local governments combined
2009–10

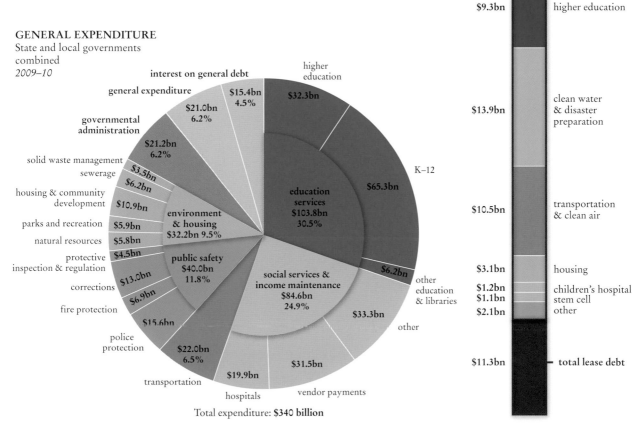

STATE DEBT
and its purposes
2012

Total expenditure: **$340 billion**

MILITARY POWER

California is the most militarized of states. It has been a strategic intellectual and technological center for the military, and served as the Pacific base of operations in several major wars.

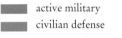

DEFENSE PERSONNEL
Number and type of personnel in top five states
2009

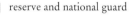

- active military
- civilian defense
- reserve and national guard

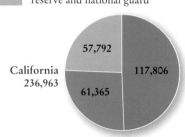

California
236,963

57,792
117,806
61,365

Texas
235,972

56,367
131,548
48,057

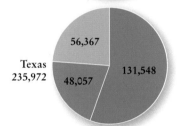

Virginia
177,982

25,109
63,160
89,713

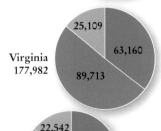

North Carolina
159,041

22,542
20,426
116,073

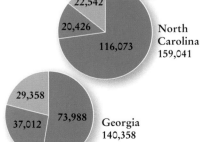

Georgia
140,358

29,358
37,012
73,988

C alifornia is the Pacific coast bulwark of American military power. It has more installations—Air Force, Army, Navy, and Marines—and more military personnel than any other state, which together form the largest complex of military bases, command and training centers, weapons stations, logistics, and operational centers in the world.

California provides a unique combination of weather, climate, and terrain, with large restricted airspace contiguous to military desert lands and mountainous terrain, and deep-water access for strategic joint training of military forces. Its technology, industry, and research universities make critical intellectual and commercial contributions to the military. With close to $40 billion in annual spending by the Department of Defense in the state, defense is one of the state's largest economic sectors.

San Francisco became the western headquarters for the Army and Navy after statehood. Indian Wars were directed out of the Presidio and the Bay became a "naval lake" through the 20th century, as did San Diego Bay when the Navy's Pacific fleet moved there in 1919. During the era of military modernization (1903–18), the Bay Area served as a key base for introducing war technologies such as ship-to-shore radio.

World War II (1939–45) turned the Bay Area into the logistical hub of the Pacific, and Los Angeles into the world's greatest aircraft production center. California also became the leader in missiles and electronics (such as radar and guidance systems). The Marines established a West Coast base at Camp Pendleton and the Air Force and Navy created huge bases for flight and ordnance testing all around Southern California. California was also the base of operations for the Korean War (1950–53) and Vietnam War (1960–75).

By the 1990s the nature of war had changed and many California bases were closed under four rounds of BRAC (Base Realignment and Closure). Southern California took a big hit from loss of defense spending and every base but one closed in the Bay Area. In the era of electronic warfare, California makes guidance systems for Predator drones and Cruise missiles.

Military expenditure by the USA shot up again in the 2000s with the wars in Afghanistan and Iraq, and further worldwide commitments. While California's share of military personnel and spending has declined from its Cold War peak of over 20 percent in the 1980s, it continues to be the largest recipient of defense contracts among all the states.

CALIFORNIA'S SHARE OF MILITARY RESOURCES
Military expenditure and active military personnel in California as percentage of US total
1994–2010

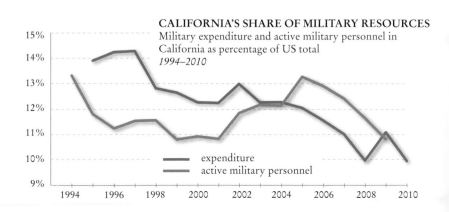

- expenditure
- active military personnel

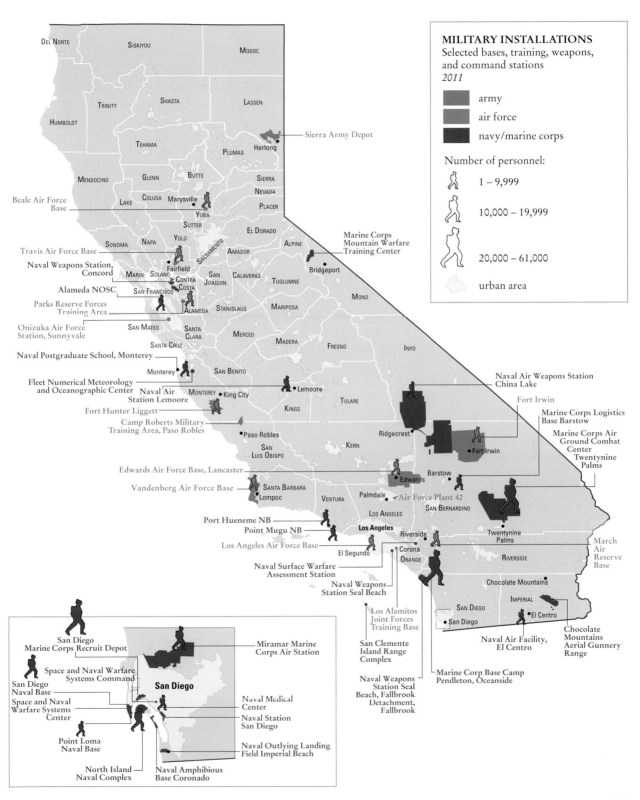

MILITARY INSTALLATIONS
Selected bases, training, weapons, and command stations
2011

army

air force

navy/marine corps

Number of personnel:

1 – 9,999

10,000 – 19,999

20,000 – 61,000

urban area

Del Norte
Siskiyou
Modoc
Trinity
Shasta
Lassen
Humboldt
Tehama
Plumas
Herlong
Sierra Army Depot
Mendocino
Glenn
Butte
Sierra
Nevada
Lake
Colusa
Marysville
Placer
Yuba
Sonoma
Napa
Yolo
Sutter
El Dorado
Alpine
Sacramento
Amador
Marine Corps Mountain Warfare Training Center
Beale Air Force Base
Fairfield
Calaveras
Bridgeport
Travis Air Force Base
San Joaquin
Tuolumne
Naval Weapons Station, Concord
Marin
Solano
Contra Costa
Mono
Alameda NOSC
San Francisco
Alameda
Stanislaus
Parks Reserve Forces Training Area
San Mateo
Santa Clara
Mariposa
Merced
Onizuka Air Force Station, Sunnyvale
Santa Cruz
Madera
Fresno
Inyo
Naval Postgraduate School, Monterey
Monterey
San Benito
Naval Air Weapons Station China Lake
Fleet Numerical Meteorology and Oceanographic Center
Monterey
Lemoore
Fort Irwin
Naval Air Station Lemoore
King City
Tulare
Marine Corps Logistics Base Barstow
Fort Hunter Liggett
Kings
Ridgecrest
Marine Corps Air Ground Combat Center Twentynine Palms
Camp Roberts Military Training Area, Paso Robles
Paso Robles
San Luis Obispo
Kern
Fort Irwin
Edwards Air Force Base, Lancaster
Edwards
Barstow
Vandenberg Air Force Base
Santa Barbara
Lompoc
Ventura
Palmdale
San Bernardino
March Air Reserve Base
Air Force Plant 42
Los Angeles
Port Hueneme NB
Twentynine Palms
Point Mugu NB
Los Angeles
Riverside
Los Angeles Air Force Base
El Segundo
Corona
Orange
Chocolate Mountains
Naval Surface Warfare Assessment Station
Riverside
Imperial
Naval Weapons Station Seal Beach
San Diego
El Centro
Los Alamitos Joint Forces Training Base
San Diego
Chocolate Mountains Aerial Gunnery Range
San Clemente Island Range Complex
Naval Air Facility, El Centro
Naval Weapons Station Seal Beach, Fallbrook Detachment, Fallbrook
Marine Corp Base Camp Pendleton, Oceanside

San Diego Marine Corps Recruit Depot
Miramar Marine Corps Air Station
Space and Naval Warfare Systems Command
San Diego Naval Base
San Diego
Space and Naval Warfare Systems Center
Point Loma Naval Base
Naval Medical Center
Naval Station San Diego
North Island Naval Complex
Naval Amphibious Base Coronado
Naval Outlying Landing Field Imperial Beach

39

CRIME & INCARCERATION

California's prison population and funding for corrections have soared in the last 30 years, even though violent crime rates have dropped. The US Supreme Court has ordered a reduction in the state's prison population to reduce overcrowding.

Until recently, California had the largest prison population in the USA; now it is second only to Texas. Figures available in 2013 indicated that, along with the incarceration of close to 150,000 people in 33 state prisons, the state held nearly 80,000 people in county jails. In addition, there are roughly 110,000 people on parole and 270,000 people on probation.

California's state prison population, which hovered around 20,000 for more than a century, exploded after 1980, rising more than eight-fold to a high of over 170,000 in 2006. This mirrored a similar, but less steep, growth of prisoners across the USA. During this period, violent crime rates declined, property crime rates remained steady, but incarceration for drug crimes soared. Since the 1980s, the funding for the Department of Corrections has grown 16 times, and its share of the general budget has increased more than any other category. Since 1980, 22 prisons have been built (as opposed to 12 in the preceding 130 years). These are mostly located in poor, inland, and northern areas, where local officials welcome them—even though they create almost no local benefits.

California's incarceration rate first began ballooning following Richard Nixon's call for a War on Drugs in 1971. In 1977, California's Determinate Sentencing Law (DSL) eliminated rehabilitation as a goal of sentencing and leant towards incarceration. During the 1980s a series of increasingly punitive "tough on crime" laws were passed, such as the Anti-Drug Abuse Act of 1986, which established mandatory minimum prison sentences for drug distribution. Over the same period, anti-drug funding to government agencies increased exponentially, while programs for drug treatment, prevention, and education were dramatically cut.

In 1994, Californians voted for the "Three Strikes" initiative, mandating life imprisonment for many three-time offenders, petty or otherwise. In 2012, the electorate moderated this punitive law, imposing a life sentence only when a new felony conviction is serious or violent.

Crime and incarceration policies have disproportionately affected men, people of color, and the unemployed. By the early 1990s, a quarter of young African-American men were under the authority of the criminal justice system. In 2010, the ratio of the rate of incarceration for Hispanics and Whites was 1.7 to 1 and an astounding 7.9 to 1 for Blacks and Whites.

RACIAL DISPARITY
Incarceration per 100,000 in population
1980–2010

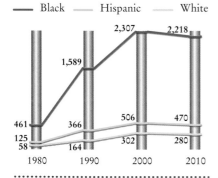

CRIME AND PUNISHMENT
Rate per 100,000 in population
in selected states
2009

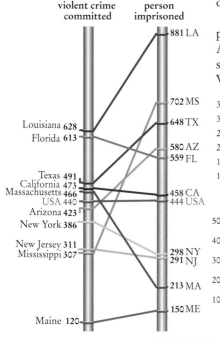

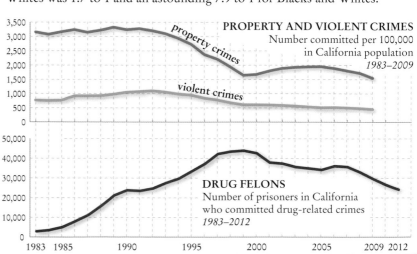

PROPERTY AND VIOLENT CRIMES
Number committed per 100,000
in California population
1983–2009

DRUG FELONS
Number of prisoners in California
who committed drug-related crimes
1983–2012

Since 1980, California's prison population has exceeded the design capacity of the system, leading to intense overcrowding. In 2001, prisoners sued the state through the Eighth Amendment's Cruel and Unusual Punishment Clause because their basic health needs were not being met. Prison inmates bear a high burden of chronic diseases, such as asthma and hypertension, as well as infectious diseases, such as hepatitis and tuberculosis. About two-thirds report drug abuse or dependency, and more than 30,000 prisoners suffer from serious mental health problems. In 2011, the US Supreme Court upheld a lower court order for a reduction in the state prison population to 137.5 percent of design capacity. This has reversed the upward trend, while recent legislation and executive action have shifted responsibility for non-serious offenders to the counties.

"Indeed, it is an uncontested fact that, on average, an inmate in one of California's prisons needlessly dies every six to seven days due to constitutional deficiencies in the medical delivery system."
– US Judge Thelton Henderson, 2005

STATE PRISON OVERCROWDING
1976–2011

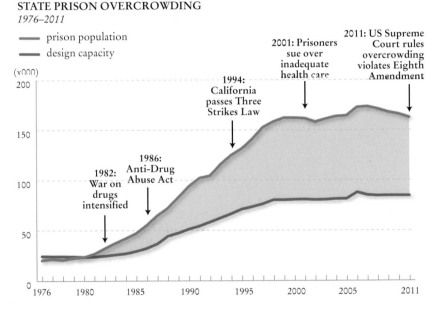

— prison population
— design capacity

(x000)

1982: War on drugs intensified

1986: Anti-Drug Abuse Act

1994: California passes Three Strikes Law

2001: Prisoners sue over inadequate health care

2011: US Supreme Court rules overcrowding violates Eighth Amendment

FUNDING FOR CORRECTIONS
As percentage of state expenditures

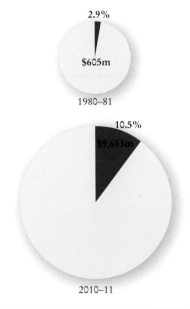

2.9%
$605m
1980–81

10.5%
$9,613m
2010–11

CAPITAL PUNISHMENT IN CALIFORNIA

California is one of 33 states in the US that, at the beginning of 2013, allowed the death penalty, with 725 inmates on death row.

In November 2012, California defeated Proposition 34, thereby retaining the death penalty. The proposition would also have

allowed persons guilty of murder to work in prison to pay for victim restitution fees.

○ legal actions   🪨 lethal gas
○ executions   💉 lethal injection

1972: California Supreme Court found death penalty in violation of State Constitution.

1973: California electorate amended State Constitution, overturning Supreme Court ruling.

1978: Voters approve death penalty statute.

1986: Voters recall three justices opposed to death penalty.

1994: Lethal gas ruled "cruel and unusual punishment" and banned.

Proposition 34 defeated, thereby retaining the death penalty.

1972 | 1973 | 1978 | 1986 | 1992 (1) | 1993 (1) | 1994 | 1996 (2) | 1998 (1) | 1999 (2) | 2000 (1) | 2001 (1) | 2002 (1) | 2005 (2) | 2006 (1) | 2012

41

Chapter Three

ECONOMY & INDUSTRY

California is one of the world's economic success stories, having every advantage and making the best of them. It entered the modern world bearing gold and has profited from an abundance of natural riches. But what counts is that Californians have continued to spin new forms of gold from investment, innovation, and opportunity for millions of people.

Technology and how to win in the arena of global competition are the hot topics in contemporary discussions of economic growth, and no place is better known for its high-tech industries than California, particularly Silicon Valley. It continues to spawn earth-shaking technologies, from medical instruments to social media, and to pull great minds into its gravitational field, where their chances of success are the greatest.

With rapid economic growth and innovation, California has gestated thousands of new businesses and supported the expansion of successful companies. In older lines are such behemoths as Chevron, Disney, and Hewlett-Packard, while recent high-tech companies like Apple, Google, and Twitter have taken the world by storm. California is still where eager entrepreneurs flock to from the four corners of the world to find investors willing to launch new ventures.

Yet, despite the attention to technology and entrepreneurship, the foundation of California's economic prosperity has been its labor force. This term conjures up visions of blue collars and factories, but it includes a wide spectrum of workers—from offices and laboratories to building sites and fields. California has never been a classic industrial state, and it has been repeatedly blessed with infusions of large numbers of well-educated and skilled workers, as well as millions of ordinary folk willing to work hard to achieve their dreams.

Agriculture has been one of California's crown jewels, and it reveals better than any other sector the paradoxes of the state's good fortune. It has turned good soil, water, and sunshine into a profusion of crops and a powerful array of products reaching markets far and wide. Here, agriculture became agribusiness and drove productivity to unseen heights, just like any other industry, but it exploited immigrant farm workers with a ferocity greater than that of any other sector.

But the California economy has not been performing as well as in the past, despite the recent glories of high tech and movie making. Growth has hit some nasty bumps in the road and slowed up badly in the 2000s. This has left too many workers unemployed and underpaid, governments short of revenues, and businesses stumbling, and underpins a host of other misfortunes afflicting the Golden State.

Server farms (data centers) are key nodes in the infrastructure of modern industry and communications.

Economic Growth

California's economic growth has long outpaced the rest of the country. With its vibrant and diverse industrial tapestry, it is a model of economic innovation and prosperity.

California is an economic titan, its GDP ranking alongside European countries and ahead of Canada and Mexico. From the 1850s onwards, it grew more rapidly than the rest of the country, boasting the largest state economy by the 1960s. Its leading positions in manufacturing, high technology, entertainment, and logistics, coupled with its advanced research and higher education systems, have contributed to an enviable status as one of the world's key industrial centers.

California has a highly diversified economy—virtually a nation unto itself. Resource extraction was the foundation of growth up to World War II, but capital from this natural wealth was invested in everything from railroads to radios, machinery to electricity. Because of its size and strategic position on the Pacific coast, the state became strong in trade and transport, and in the 20th century it became a leader in utilities and construction. Manufacturing grew as a complement to mining, agriculture, and transportation, but only became a primary driver of growth in the mid-20th century, led by aerospace (California became the largest manufacturing state circa 1970).

The state's largest basic industries today are electronics (computing, internet, social media), entertainment (films, TV, recording), oil and refining, chemicals, and food products. There are many other vibrant sectors, as well, such as machinery, metalworking, aerospace, garments, and printing. Many industries are geographically concentrated and popularly identified with specific places, especially Silicon Valley (electronics) and Hollywood (entertainment). California's consumer-serving sectors—retailing, health, and restaurants—thrive because of high average incomes and tourists flocking to places like San Francisco, Disneyland, and Yosemite.

Economic growth has come in spectacular waves, such as the silver and railroad boom of the 1860s, the citrus and fruit mania of the 1880s, and the oil and auto bubble of the 1920s. World War II brought a huge expansion of aircraft, shipbuilding, and military electronics, and the postwar era saw massive growth in highways, water projects, education, and construction.

California was hard hit in the last three downturns: 1989–91, 2000–01 and 2008–10. Its economy peaked as the world's fifth largest in 1999, but sluggish growth in the 2000s has taken the glow off its past accomplishments. Meanwhile, China and other rising nations have overtaken many developed areas like California in growth rates and size.

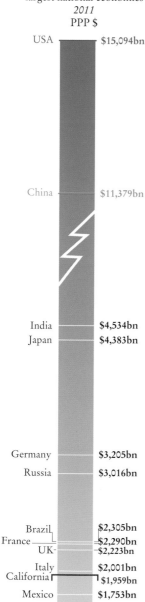

TOP ECONOMIES
Gross Domestic Product of California
compared to that of
largest national economies
2011
PPP $

USA	$15,094bn
China	$11,379bn
India	$4,534bn
Japan	$4,383bn
Germany	$3,205bn
Russia	$3,016bn
Brazil	$2,305bn
France	$2,290bn
UK	$2,223bn
Italy	$2,001bn
California	$1,959bn
Mexico	$1,753bn

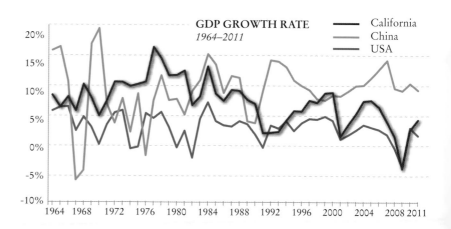

GDP GROWTH RATE
1964–2011

— California
— China
— USA

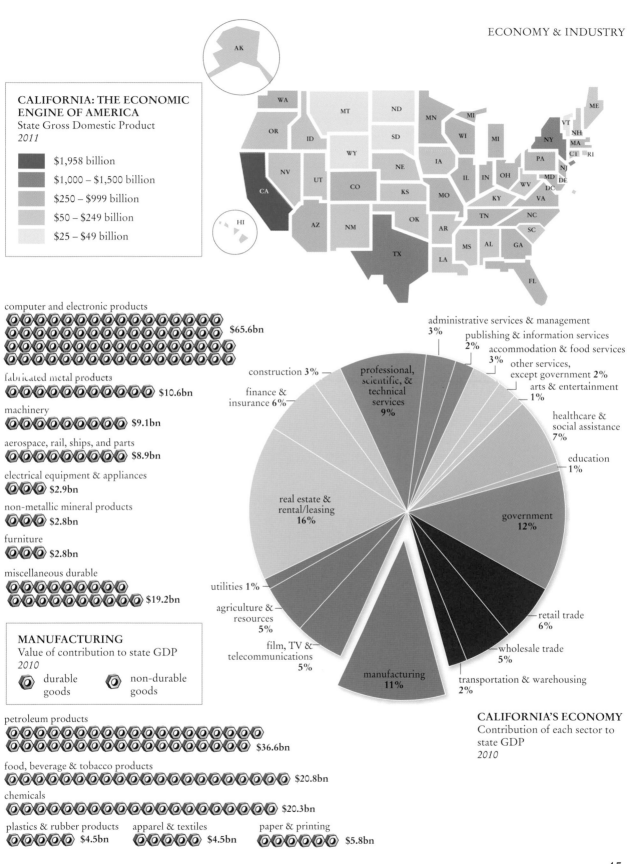

CALIFORNIA: THE ECONOMIC ENGINE OF AMERICA
State Gross Domestic Product
2011

- $1,958 billion
- $1,000 – $1,500 billion
- $250 – $999 billion
- $50 – $249 billion
- $25 – $49 billion

computer and electronic products
$65.6bn

fabricated metal products
$10.6bn

machinery
$9.1bn

aerospace, rail, ships, and parts
$8.9bn

electrical equipment & appliances
$2.9bn

non-metallic mineral products
$2.8bn

furniture
$2.8bn

miscellaneous durable
$19.2bn

MANUFACTURING
Value of contribution to state GDP
2010
durable goods   non-durable goods

petroleum products
$36.6bn

food, beverage & tobacco products
$20.8bn

chemicals
$20.3bn

plastics & rubber products   apparel & textiles   paper & printing
$4.5bn $4.5bn $5.8bn

administrative services & management 3%
publishing & information services 2%
accommodation & food services 3%
other services, except government 2%
arts & entertainment 1%
healthcare & social assistance 7%
education 1%
government 12%
retail trade 6%
wholesale trade 5%
transportation & warehousing 2%
manufacturing 11%
film, TV & telecommunications 5%
agriculture & resources 5%
utilities 1%
real estate & rental/leasing 16%
finance & insurance 6%
construction 3%
professional, scientific, & technical services 9%

CALIFORNIA'S ECONOMY
Contribution of each sector to state GDP
2010

45

WORKFORCE

California's prosperity has been built on its workforce, both in numbers and quality. Labor demand and supply, skills, and wages have long exceeded the national average, feeding the state's remarkable growth.

California's labor force is the largest of any state, at 18.4 million, or roughly 12 percent of the US labor force. Its growth outpaced the rest of the country for decades, and the migration of millions of workers to the state fed economic expansion. But job creation flattened out in the 2000s and, during the Great Recession, the unemployment rate stayed over 10 percent for four years (over 20 percent in some interior counties), peaking at 12.3 percent or 2.2 million people out of work.

Wages started out very high in 19th-century California and remain roughly 15 percent higher than the US average, fifth among the states. High wages meant that California workers were good consumers, fueling robust markets for locally produced goods. There are large geographic, educational, and racial disparities in wages, however. While skilled labor garners a premium in the high-tech economy, ordinary workers—mostly women and people of color—have suffered from stagnant wages.

California has always benefited from a high proportion of educated, trained workers in the labor force. They have fed the economy's appetite for skilled labor, which has, in turn, contributed to high productivity and innovation in industry, as well as to high-quality research, education, and healthcare to sustain an innovative economy. But less-prepared workers have always been needed in large numbers to fill low-skill, low-wage jobs—which have proliferated in recent years.

AVERAGE WEEKLY WAGE
Selected states
2011

New York	$1,188
Connecticut	$1,176
Massachusetts	$1,148
New Jersey	$1,107
California	$1,058
Maryland	$1,019
Illinois	$978
US average	$924
Mississippi	$673

LABOR FORCE GROWTH
California compared to USA
1971–2011

California (x millions)
USA (x 10 millions)

- California labor force
- California total employed
- US labor force
- US total employed
- unemployed labor force

California's mix of jobs reflects its economic complexity and richness. Several of the fastest-growing occupations cluster in healthcare, technology, and management, including home-health aides, paramedics, biochemists, nurses, database administrators, software developers, and marketing analysts. The demand for low-skill labor in restaurants, home care, sales, and office work is projected to be robust due to the high rate of retirement of baby boomers, and growth in retail, personal services, and business services.

Over 2 million California workers belong to unions. Unionization in California, as in the USA, has been falling for several decades, but has always stood above the national average and has held steady in the last decade. The strength of the union movement today lies in the healthcare and public sectors, where workers were not allowed to unionize until the 1960s and are under political pressure today.

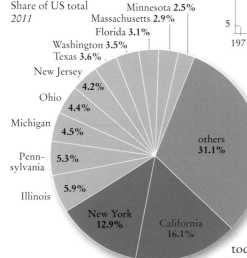

UNION MEMBERSHIP
Share of US total
2011

- Minnesota 2.5%
- Massachusetts 2.9%
- Florida 3.1%
- Washington 3.5%
- Texas 3.6%
- New Jersey 4.2%
- Ohio 4.4%
- Michigan 4.5%
- Pennsylvania 5.3%
- Illinois 5.9%
- New York 12.9%
- California 16.1%
- others 31.1%

Total membership: 14,765,000

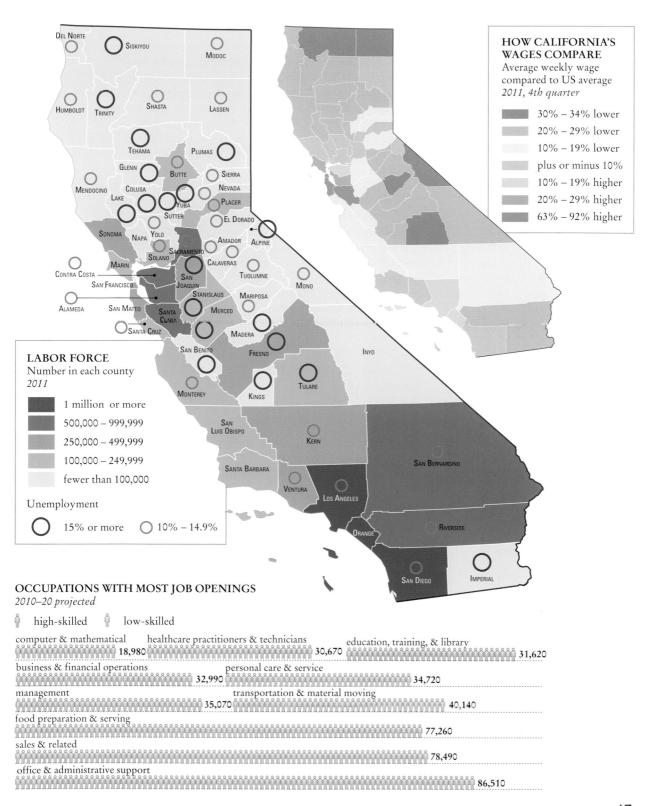

HOW CALIFORNIA'S WAGES COMPARE
Average weekly wage compared to US average
2011, 4th quarter

- 30% – 34% lower
- 20% – 29% lower
- 10% – 19% lower
- plus or minus 10%
- 10% – 19% higher
- 20% – 29% higher
- 63% – 92% higher

LABOR FORCE
Number in each county
2011

- 1 million or more
- 500,000 – 999,999
- 250,000 – 499,999
- 100,000 – 249,999
- fewer than 100,000

Unemployment

- ◯ 15% or more
- ◯ 10% – 14.9%

OCCUPATIONS WITH MOST JOB OPENINGS
2010–20 projected

high-skilled   low-skilled

computer & mathematical   18,980
healthcare practitioners & technicians   30,670
education, training, & library   31,620
business & financial operations   32,990
personal care & service   34,720
management   35,070
transportation & material moving   40,140
food preparation & serving   77,260
sales & related   78,490
office & administrative support   86,510

47

BUSINESS & FINANCE

California is home not only to globe-straddling corporations with large management teams, but also to thriving small businesses and start-ups. It has long been the second-largest center of finance in the country.

California's economy is anchored by the many large corporations that have grown up with the state's industries and are still headquartered here: 53 of the Fortune 500, more than any other state. These include household names such as Hewlett-Packard and Disney, and many less well-known giants such as Qualcomm and McKesson. Some very large firms, such as Bechtel, are privately owned and do not appear in the Fortune list. Many, including Chevron and Apple, are global concerns with far-flung networks of supply, distribution, management, and sales.

California has been a land of business opportunity since the Gold Rush and nurtures far more new companies every year than any other state. While Silicon Valley is justly famous for its culture of start-ups, Los Angeles has the highest rate of new-business formation of any US metro area. The result of this entrepreneurial activity is that the average size of industrial firms and factories in California is smaller than the national average.

Business and government in California have always worked hand in hand. While California has some of the strongest regulations in the country for things such as air pollution and worker safety, many state, county, and city laws, taxes, and regulations have been adapted to the needs of industry, as in stem-cell research subsidies, mail-order sales of wine, or prorationing of oil production.

START-UPS
Number of people aged 20 – 64
who started a business
2009–11
per million in population

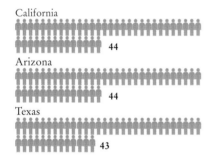

California 44

Arizona 44

Texas 43

Florida 41

New York 36

US average 33

Massachusetts 31

Ohio 28

Washington 24

Illinois 23

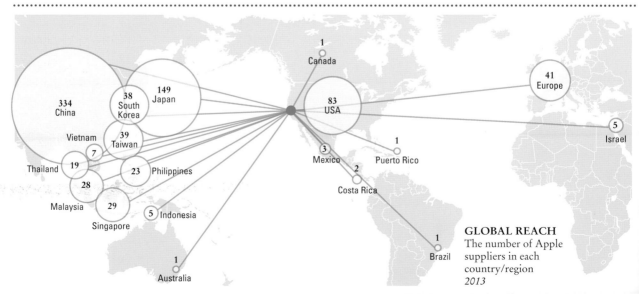

334 China
149 Japan
38 South Korea
39 Taiwan
Vietnam 7
Thailand 19
Malaysia 28
Singapore 29
Indonesia 5
Philippines 23
Australia 1

Canada 1
USA 83
Mexico 3
Costa Rica 2
Puerto Rico 1
Brazil 1

Europe 41
Israel 5

GLOBAL REACH
The number of Apple suppliers in each country/region
2013

Modern business firms require professional management, backed by a variety of business services, including accounting, law, engineering, and design. California has long had a flourishing business and administrative services sector, mostly concentrated in the centers of big cities, serving companies of every sort: industrial, mercantile, transportation, agribusiness, film, or finance. This has meant that the state has a high proportion of office workers, many of whom are highly skilled and well paid.

California hosts a large financial sector that includes banks such as Wells Fargo, the credit-card system manager VISA, and the mutual fund giant Pimco. It is also home to a host of lesser known but important financial operators, such as private equity (investment) firm KKR and the immense index fund trader, Blackrock. Lastly, it boasts the world's biggest cluster of venture capital firms.

Financiers are mostly located in downtown San Francisco and Los Angeles, or in upscale suburbs such as Newport Beach, San Mateo, and Menlo Park. California institutions introduced several key financial innovations, such as the Visa and Mastercard systems and online stock trading. But the state has generated many financial excesses, such as the subprime mortgage mania behind the housing bubble that burst in 2008, unleashing huge financial losses for bankers and homeowners.

BANKING DEPOSITS
States with highest deposits
2009

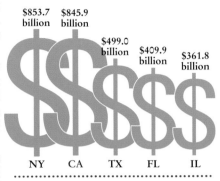

$853.7 billion NY · $845.9 billion CA · $499.0 billion TX · $409.9 billion FL · $361.8 billion IL

BIG BUSINESS
The 25 largest California corporations in the Fortune 500 according to value of sales
2012
sales shown in $ billions

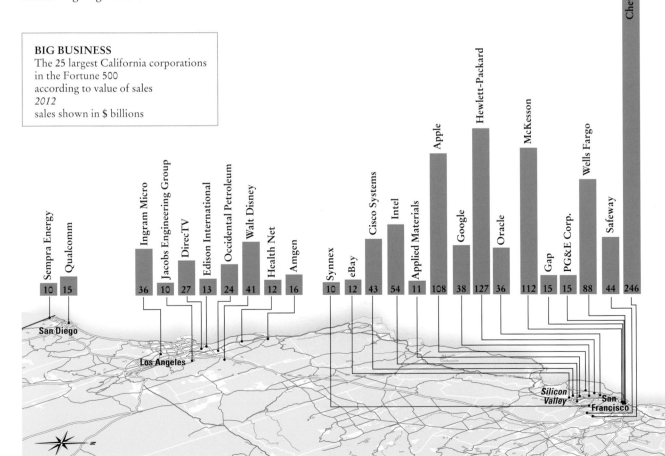

AGRIBUSINESS

California's agribusiness is one of the agricultural wonders of the world, leading the country in the variety and quantity of output, and setting the pace for modern farming and food production in the United States.

MAJOR CALIFORNIAN CROPS
Percentage of total cash income from farming *2011*

- fruit & nuts **35%**
- livestock & animal products **28%**
- vegetables **17%**
- field crops **11%**
- horticulture **8.5%**

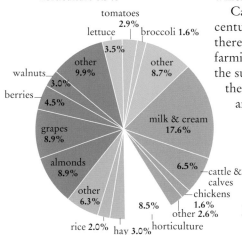

tomatoes **2.9%**
lettuce **3.5%**
broccoli **1.6%**
other **9.9%**
other **8.7%**
walnuts **3.0%**
berries **4.5%**
grapes **8.9%**
milk & cream **17.6%**
almonds **8.9%**
6.5%
other **6.3%**
cattle & calves
chickens **1.6%**
rice **2.0%**
hay **3.0%**
8.5%
other **2.6%**
horticulture

Total cash income from sales: $43.5 billion

MAJOR DESTINATIONS OF AGRICULTURAL EXPORTS
Approximate export value *2010*

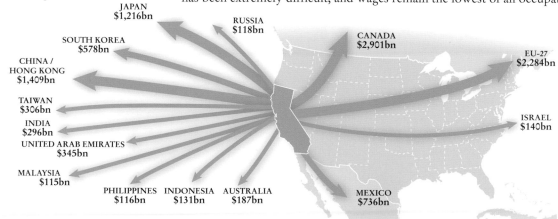

JAPAN **$1,216bn**
RUSSIA **$118bn**
CANADA **$2,901bn**
EU-27 **$2,284bn**
SOUTH KOREA **$578bn**
CHINA / HONG KONG **$1,409bn**
TAIWAN **$306bn**
INDIA **$296bn**
UNITED ARAB EMIRATES **$345bn**
ISRAEL **$140bn**
MALAYSIA **$115bn**
PHILIPPINES **$116bn**
INDONESIA **$131bn**
AUSTRALIA **$187bn**
MEXICO **$736bn**

California's agricultural output is prodigious: over $43 billion per year in sales of over 400 types of plant and animal crops. Farm output is half as large again as the next largest state and no other part of the US comes close to California's variety. The full array of agribusiness—inputs, transport, and processing—generates triple the revenue of on-farm production alone, amounting to nearly 10 percent of state GDP.

Agriculture passed mining as California's leading sector after 1875, and led the US by 1925. It is characterized by professional management, large-scale operations, and capital-intensive methods, yielding high productivity and profits. It is also notorious for intense exploitation of farm workers, most of whom are immigrants. Agribusiness reaches far beyond the farm. Key inputs are seeds and stock, fertilizer, machinery, and animal feed. California led the way in developing petrochemical fertilizers and pesticides, as well as industrial henhouses for chickens, confined feeding of milk cows, and feedlots for cattle. Agribusiness extends to shippers and cooperatives, which have been brilliant marketers of everything from oranges to almonds.

California became the country's largest producer of dried fruit in the 19th century, canned goods in the early 20th, and fresh fruits and vegetables thereafter. Food processors like Del Monte Corporation invented contract farming to supply their canneries. Grocery chains, such as Ralphs, perfected the supermarket in the 1920s, and McDonald's created the fast-food chain in the 1950s. Today, California is a prodigious exporter of specialty products around the world.

In making the land productive, growers have literally moved mountains, rearranging the landscape by redirecting rivers, draining thousands of acres of wetlands, and flattening fields as far as the eye can see. They have drenched the land with more pesticides than anywhere on Earth, endangering farm workers and consumers, and have left a persistent legacy of air and water pollution from fertilizers, leaching of salts and metals, and soil erosion.

Over 400,000 farm workers toil in the fields, often many more at peak season. Most farm workers are of Mexican origin and a large number are unauthorized. The social order of rural California is ruled by the growers and their allies. Their reach extends into the big cities, where many are headquartered and have close ties to financiers, merchants, and processors. Their collective power extends deep into state government. Labor organizing has been extremely difficult, and wages remain the lowest of all occupations.

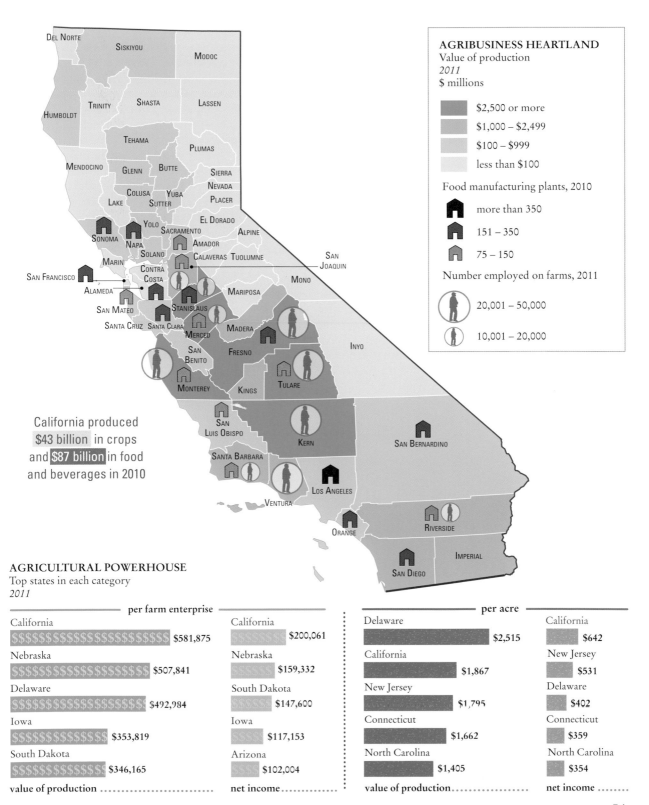

AGRIBUSINESS HEARTLAND
Value of production
2011
$ millions

$2,500 or more
$1,000 – $2,499
$100 – $999
less than $100

Food manufacturing plants, 2010

more than 350
151 – 350
75 – 150

Number employed on farms, 2011

20,001 – 50,000
10,001 – 20,000

California produced
$43 billion in crops
and $87 billion in food
and beverages in 2010

AGRICULTURAL POWERHOUSE
Top states in each category
2011

per farm enterprise			
California		California	
$581,875		$200,061	
Nebraska		Nebraska	
$507,841		$159,332	
Delaware		South Dakota	
$492,984		$147,600	
Iowa		Iowa	
$353,819		$117,153	
South Dakota		Arizona	
$346,165		$102,004	
value of production		net income	

per acre			
Delaware		California	
$2,515		$642	
California		New Jersey	
$1,867		$531	
New Jersey		Delaware	
$1,795		$402	
Connecticut		Connecticut	
$1,662		$359	
North Carolina		North Carolina	
$1,405		$354	
value of production		net income	

TECHNOLOGY

California is known around the world as a leader in technology and innovation. It has offered highly favorable conditions for innovators to flourish and put new ideas into play.

California is at the leading edge of technological innovation. Silicon Valley is the world center of high-tech, spawning products that have changed the world—personal computers, internet searches, tweets, and smart phones—and home to some of the most famous names in high-tech, including four of the five largest internet portals (Google, Facebook, YouTube, and Yahoo) and the leading popular electronics company (Apple).

California has long pushed the technology envelope. It launched a revolution in mining in the 19th century, then in oil drilling and refining in the 20th. It was a pioneer in electricity with the modern turbine and long-distance transmission, and in construction with reinforced concrete and the high-arch dam. California changed aeronautics with the single-wing plane. The vacuum tube was invented here, as were television and radar tubes, and the integrated circuit. Several new breeds of plants and animals were developed in California, such as the Idaho potato. So were some of the first industrial foods, such as the canned olive, and first fast-food chains, like Denny's and Taco Bell. Gene splicing and genetically modified organisms emerged in California, giving birth to the world's largest concentration of biotechnology research and enterprise. New medical technologies, such as open-heart surgery, were developed here.

Why have Californians been so innovative? A key reason is an abundance of young, skilled, and creative people; California has drawn some of the best minds from around the world and has been a leader in public education, and it gave enterprising people the opportunity to put their ideas to work. The uptake of inventions has been aided by abundant capital (including the nation's largest venture capital pool); by thriving markets for new goods because of the state's prosperity; and by large amounts invested in basic and applied research, especially by government grants to the state's major universities, medical schools, and defense contractors.

Technological innovation has been essential to California's rapid economic growth. It raised productivity through the use of new machinery and mass-production methods, helping to keep wages and incomes high, and introduced new products that allowed businesses to proliferate. Yet there are troubling signs amidst the success stories. California's productivity leadership has declined and Silicon Valley tech firms have led the way in using temporary labor and offshore suppliers who undercut local workers. Global competition in electronics is growing, with countries pouring money into research, education, and high-end production facilities.

PATENTS GRANTED WORLDWIDE
Highest totals
1963–2011

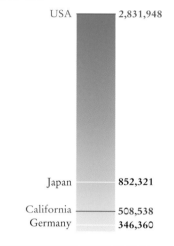

USA	2,831,948
Japan	852,321
California	508,538
Germany	346,360

SHARE OF US PATENTS
By state
2011

Total: 108,499

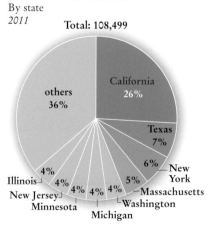

California 26%
others 36%
Texas 7%
New York 6%
Massachusetts 5%
Washington 4%
Michigan 4%
Minnesota 4%
New Jersey 4%
Illinois 4%

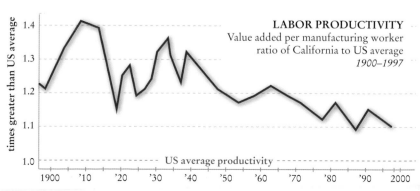

LABOR PRODUCTIVITY
Value added per manufacturing worker
ratio of California to US average
1900–1997

times greater than US average

US average productivity

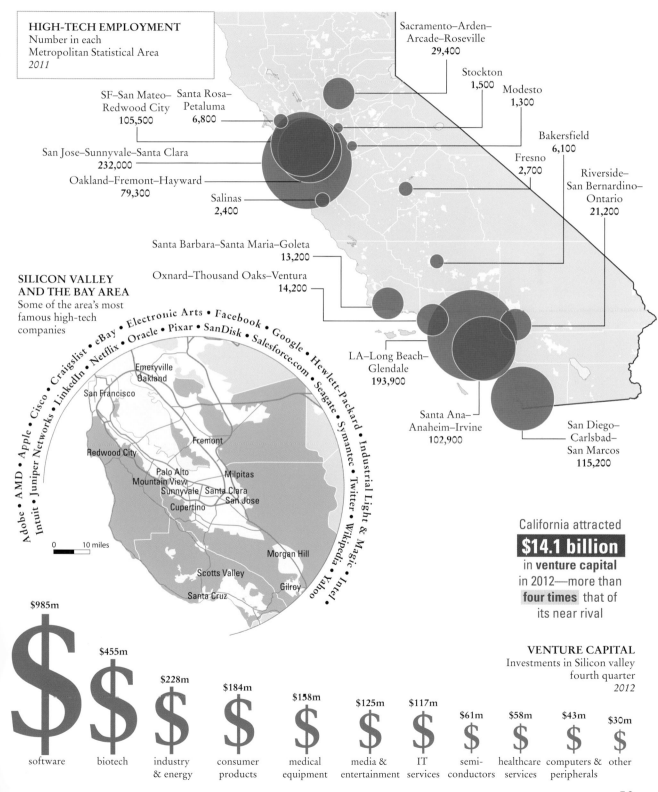

HIGH-TECH EMPLOYMENT
Number in each
Metropolitan Statistical Area
2011

Sacramento–Arden–
Arcade–Roseville
29,400

Stockton
1,500

Modesto
1,300

SF–San Mateo–
Redwood City
105,500

Santa Rosa–
Petaluma
6,800

Bakersfield
6,100

Fresno
2,700

San Jose–Sunnyvale–Santa Clara
232,000

Riverside–
San Bernardino–
Ontario
21,200

Oakland–Fremont–Hayward
79,300

Salinas
2,400

**SILICON VALLEY
AND THE BAY AREA**
Some of the area's most
famous high-tech
companies

Santa Barbara–Santa Maria–Goleta
13,200

Oxnard–Thousand Oaks–Ventura
14,200

LA–Long Beach–
Glendale
193,900

Adobe • AMD • Apple • Cisco • Craigslist • eBay • Electronic Arts • Facebook • Google • Hewlett-Packard • Industrial Light & Magic • Intel • Juniper Networks • LinkedIn • Netflix • Oracle • Pixar • SanDisk • Salesforce.com • Seagate • Symantec • Twitter • Wikipedia • Yahoo

Emeryville
Oakland

San Francisco

Fremont

Redwood City

Palo Alto
Mountain View
Sunnyvale   Santa Clara
Cupertino   San Jose

Milpitas

Morgan Hill

Scotts Valley

Gilroy

Santa Cruz

0   10 miles

Santa Ana–
Anaheim–Irvine
102,900

San Diego–
Carlsbad–
San Marcos
115,200

California attracted

$14.1 billion

in **venture capital**
in 2012—more than
four times that of
its near rival

VENTURE CAPITAL
Investments in Silicon valley
fourth quarter
2012

$985m

$455m

$228m

$184m

$158m

$125m

$117m

$61m

$58m

$43m

$30m

software | biotech | industry & energy | consumer products | medical equipment | media & entertainment | IT services | semi-conductors | healthcare services | computers & peripherals | other

Chapter Four

Urban Areas

California's cities are world famous. San Francisco began as the city of gold, and has added many reputations since: beautiful, exotic, sinful, rebellious, rich. Hollywood has been an icon for a century, with its glamorous stars, brilliant talents, and brash money-making. Everyone today knows Silicon Valley and every government around the world wants to recreate its technical magic and economic fecundity. And who doesn't speak of Los Angeles in the same breath as New York, Paris, or Singapore? LA was even declared "the capital of the 20th century" by some scholars not long ago.

Cities are a geographic puzzle, no less in California. Confusion reigns about what constitutes a city. Is it a political unit? A commuting field? A way of life? There are municipalities, metropolitan areas, and more ways of setting boundaries. For urbanists, cities are defined by density of settlement, concentrations of activity, and the build-up of physical structures. For ordinary people, they are where most of us live, work, and play; in a way, they are everything we experience. And in today's California, they cover huge swaths of the landscape and are home to most of the state's 38 million souls. But cities are not the same as states or nations—they are a vital subject for study and mapping in their own right.

To begin with, urban economies must be recognized for their size and power. Silicon Valley, Hollywood, Downtown San Francisco, the Miracle Mile—all should be seen as organs in the body of large cities. We regularly attribute technological innovation, thriving business startups, and blossoming profits to the genius of Steve Jobs, entrepreneurial fever, or miracles of science, but to do so is to miss the forest for the trees. The vitality and innovation of such people and places have more to do with urban labor markets, capital sources, and dense interaction than anything else.

This insight leads to the broader subject of city life, which has fascinated commentators from Victor Hugo to Ridley Scott. What is it about the culture of cities and unexpected encounters that trigger delight and inventiveness among human beings? Conversely, what is it about cities that repels, and has led so many people to escape to suburban enclaves full of others like themselves? Cities are places of coming together, but they also fly apart into a thousand pieces, which we struggle to put together into a meaningful picture.

This California suburb
is a vision of the good life
written on the landscape.

CITIES & METRO AREAS

California is highly urban, and the state's cities and metro areas are among the nation's largest, densest, and most economically significant.

California has always been an urban state; today 95 percent of its people live in cities. Over time, the biggest cities have grown into metropolitan areas that encompass many suburbs and former satellites. Los Angeles is the second most populous Metropolitan Statistical Area (MSA) in the USA. An even larger census unit is the Combined Statistical Area (CSA); Greater LA is the nation's second largest CSA and the Greater Bay Area the sixth largest.

Some California cities, such as San Diego, were established as Spanish *pueblos* before the Gold Rush. Many in the north, such as Stockton, were founded in the mining era after 1848. Some, such as Modesto, started as centers of agricultural trade and transport in the 19th century. Many more began as residential satellites like Del Mar or industrial enclaves like Vernon. Suburbs multiplied so rapidly in the 20th century that the Bay Area now has over 100 independent cities and Greater Los Angeles almost 200.

Cities are the engines of modern economic growth; they are where most businesses locate, government offices concentrate, and people work. The advantages of urban clustering are all about access: to ports and airports, workers of all kinds, customers, governments, financiers, and especially other businesses. Cities are where knowledge, talent, and new ideas come together to create innovation. The largest urban regions, such as Greater LA and the Bay Area, have economies on the scale of whole countries.

Cities are linked together by transportation and communication networks, business and personal relations, and flows of goods and labor. Although LA and San Francisco are often rivals, they have many close ties, like that between movie-making in the south and digital special effects in the north. California cities have dense linkages to other urban regions around the country and to the great cities of East Asia and Europe.

Big cities expand at their edges through accretion of residences, workplaces, and stores. Most growth over the last 20 years has taken place on the interior edges of the big metropolitan areas: the Inland Empire of Southern California and the Central Valley of Northern California. Cities also grow upward and today only New York is denser than the Los Angeles and San Francisco MSAs.

POPULATION AND GDP
Of largest US Metro Areas (MSAs) *2010*

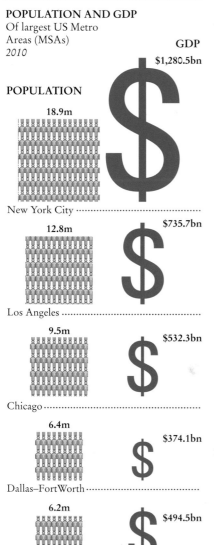

GDP

POPULATION

18.9m — $1,280.5bn
New York City

12.8m — $735.7bn
Los Angeles

9.5m — $532.3bn
Chicago

6.4m — $374.1bn
Dallas–FortWorth

6.2m — $494.5bn
Bay Area (San Francisco & San Jose)

5.9m — $384.6bn
Houston

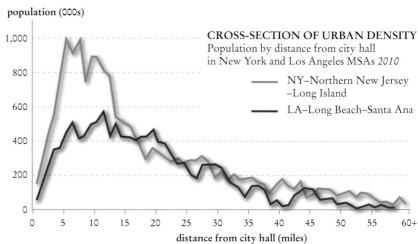

population (000s)

CROSS-SECTION OF URBAN DENSITY
Population by distance from city hall in New York and Los Angeles MSAs *2010*

— NY–Northern New Jersey –Long Island

— LA–Long Beach–Santa Ana

distance from city hall (miles)

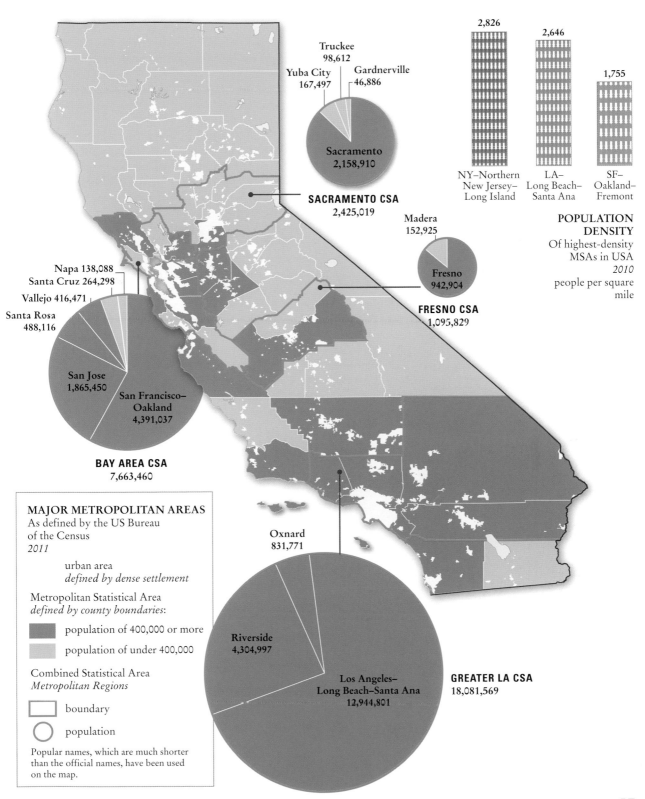

2,826

NY–Northern
New Jersey–
Long Island

2,646

LA–
Long Beach–
Santa Ana

1,755

SF–
Oakland–
Fremont

**POPULATION
DENSITY**
Of highest-density
MSAs in USA
2010
people per square
mile

Truckee
98,612

Yuba City
167,497

Gardnerville
46,886

Sacramento
2,158,910

SACRAMENTO CSA
2,425,019

Madera
152,925

Fresno
942,904

FRESNO CSA
1,095,829

Napa 138,088
Santa Cruz 264,298

Vallejo 416,471

Santa Rosa
488,116

San Jose
1,865,450

San Francisco–
Oakland
4,391,037

BAY AREA CSA
7,663,460

MAJOR METROPOLITAN AREAS
As defined by the US Bureau
of the Census
2011

    urban area
    defined by dense settlement

Metropolitan Statistical Area
defined by county boundaries:

population of 400,000 or more

population of under 400,000

Combined Statistical Area
Metropolitan Regions

    boundary

    population

Popular names, which are much shorter
than the official names, have been used
on the map.

Oxnard
831,771

Riverside
4,304,997

Los Angeles–
Long Beach–Santa Ana
12,944,801

GREATER LA CSA
18,081,569

The Bay Area

San Francisco has long been world famous, but is today part of a large, complex urban region: the Bay Area—high-tech capital of the world and richest big city in the country.

The Bay Area is the most complex urban region in the US, with three big cities and four subregions: San Francisco/West Bay, Oakland/East Bay, South Bay/Silicon Valley, and the North Bay. It is often underestimated by counting only the five-county San Francisco–Oakland metro area (population 4.3 million), not the full nine-county Bay Area (7.2 million). To confound things, San Jose has passed San Francisco in size—a unique inversion of urban primacy.

San Francisco came out of nowhere in the Gold Rush to become an international icon and the 10th largest US city by 1870. It stood alone as the capital of the Pacific Coast in the 19th century and remained the commercial and financial heart of the West until the mid-20th century, despite challenges from Seattle and Los Angeles. By 1900, Oakland had become the fastest growing part of the Bay Area, giving the region twin cities. After World War II, San Jose morphed into Silicon Valley, and the Bay Area became the only three-headed metropolis in the country. The outer East Bay and North Bay took off after 1975, and urban growth has been spilling outward ever since. Today's megapolis stretches 100 miles in every direction, merging with Sacramento and Stockton into an urbanized region over 10 million strong.

A regional manufacturing base developed around metals and machining, lumber, ships and vehicles, and food processing up to 1950. By 1975, the Bay Area had become the high-tech capital of the world, a cluster that today focuses on information technology: business software, internet equipment, security, games, and social media. The area also hosts the nation's chief concentrations of biotechnology and medical equipment, and the high-tech cluster is backed up by premier universities and medical schools at Stanford and the University of California.

The social character of the Bay Area is distinctive: evenly split between Whites and people of color, and with the highest concentration of Asians of any US urban region (almost one-quarter). High-tech rests on a large concentration of professional and technical workers, featuring the second-highest percentage of college graduates of any US city. Regional leadership in innovation draws great minds from around the world, and over half the high-tech startups in recent years were created by Chinese and Indian immigrants.

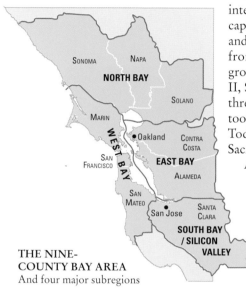

THE NINE-COUNTY BAY AREA
And four major subregions

TOP MILLIONAIRE METRO AREAS
In USA 2010

number of high net worth individuals per 1,000 in population

San Francisco & San Jose, CA
47

New York
46

Washington DC
37

Boston, MA
29

Chicago, IL
28

Detroit, MI
26

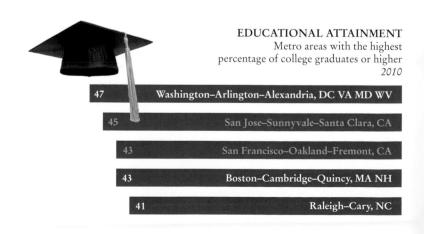

EDUCATIONAL ATTAINMENT
Metro areas with the highest percentage of college graduates or higher
2010

47	Washington–Arlington–Alexandria, DC VA MD WV
45	San Jose–Sunnyvale–Santa Clara, CA
43	San Francisco–Oakland–Fremont, CA
43	Boston–Cambridge–Quincy, MA NH
41	Raleigh–Cary, NC

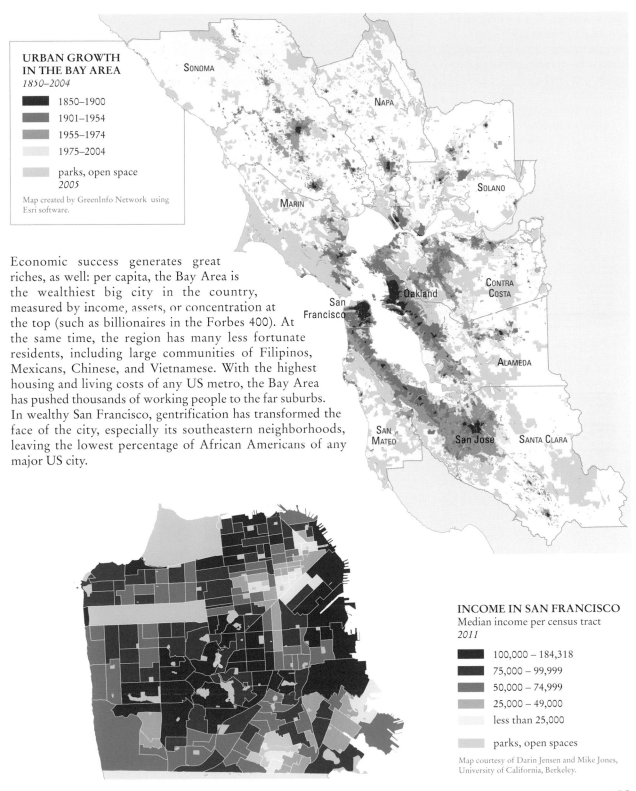

**URBAN GROWTH
IN THE BAY AREA**
1850–2004

- 1850–1900
- 1901–1954
- 1955–1974
- 1975–2004
- parks, open space
2005

Map created by GreenInfo Network using
Esri software.

Economic success generates great riches, as well: per capita, the Bay Area is the wealthiest big city in the country, measured by income, assets, or concentration at the top (such as billionaires in the Forbes 400). At the same time, the region has many less fortunate residents, including large communities of Filipinos, Mexicans, Chinese, and Vietnamese. With the highest housing and living costs of any US metro, the Bay Area has pushed thousands of working people to the far suburbs. In wealthy San Francisco, gentrification has transformed the face of the city, especially its southeastern neighborhoods, leaving the lowest percentage of African Americans of any major US city.

INCOME IN SAN FRANCISCO
Median income per census tract
2011

- 100,000 – 184,318
- 75,000 – 99,999
- 50,000 – 74,999
- 25,000 – 49,000
- less than 25,000
- parks, open spaces

Map courtesy of Darin Jensen and Mike Jones,
University of California, Berkeley.

59

GREATER LOS ANGELES

Los Angeles is California's largest city and the country's second largest metropolis. It is popularly known for its remarkable growth, sprawling landscape and mixture of peoples, but is equally a manufacturing and transportation powerhouse.

Los Angeles is the second largest city in the United States, with a population of 3.8 million, and the second most populous metropolitan region, with 18.1 million people in 2011. It is one of the world's top ten urban agglomerations. The urban region stretches across five counties, covering 10,000 square miles and extreme differences in climate, topography, and society.

Los Angeles took off in the late 19th century on the basis of oil, citrus fruits, and retirees. It kept growing rapidly throughout the 20th century: LA caught San Francisco in 1910, doubled the Bay Area by 1930, and passed Chicago as the nation's second city in the 1960s. The Inland Empire of Riverside and southern San Bernardino counties passed the 3 million mark in the 2000s.

Los Angeles city expanded by annexation, unlike San Francisco, to be one of the most spacious municipalities in the US. The suburbs spilled into the county by the 1920s, pushing west to the coast, south to Long Beach, and northeast into the San Gabriel Valley. By the 1960s, northern Orange County and the East County were the major growth peripheries, followed by Ventura and the Antelope Valley from the 1970s. Then the Inland Empire began to take off in the 1980s and became the main growth area in the 2000s.

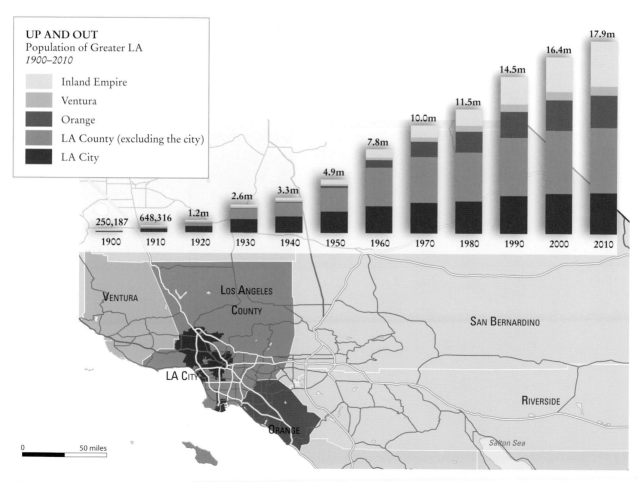

UP AND OUT
Population of Greater LA
1900–2010

- Inland Empire
- Ventura
- Orange
- LA County (excluding the city)
- LA City

0   50 miles

60

The economy of Greater LA is formidable; it is comparable in size to the top 20 countries in terms of output. Hollywood, which became the world's largest movie and entertainment production center by the 1910s, has deeply influenced local culture. Southern California became the leading aircraft manufacturing center in the 1920s, adding missiles and aerospace in the 1940s, and military electronics by the 1960s. The rest of the industrial base is diverse, including vehicles, foodstuffs, garments, building materials, metal-working, machinery, and refining. A key sector is logistics, moving a large share of American foreign trade through the ports of Los Angeles and Long Beach.

The racial make-up of Los Angeles changed dramatically in the late 20th century. The metropolis served as the main receiving area for immigrants to the US from 1975 to 2000 and is today a vibrant multicultural place. The urban landscape is a fluid checkerboard of settlements, many of them representing the largest concentrations of nationalities outside their home countries (e.g., Persians, Armenians, Mexicans). The residential pattern of national and racial groups is markedly segregated, although city life mixes peoples in surprising ways.

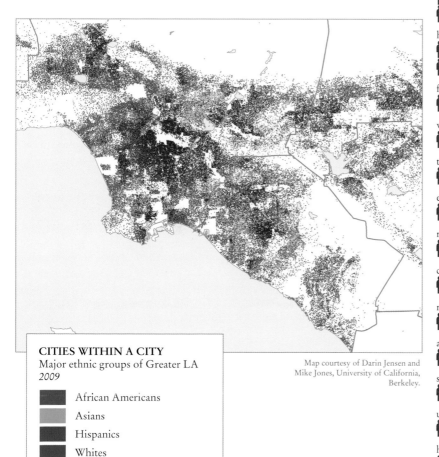

CITIES WITHIN A CITY
Major ethnic groups of Greater LA
2009

- African Americans
- Asians
- Hispanics
- Whites

Map courtesy of Darin Jensen and Mike Jones, University of California, Berkeley.

MAJOR EMPLOYMENT SECTORS
LA City
2012

restaurants & food — 605,000

management & business services — 569,000

government — 561,800

manufacturing — 519,000

retail trade (stores & dealers) — 401,400

healthcare — 361,000

finance (banks, securities, & insurance) — 217,400

wholesale trade — 210,300

transportation & warehousing — 138,300

education — 136,400

repair, personal, & other services — 136,200

construction — 107,200

real estate — 75,300

arts & entertainment — 69,600

social assistance — 60,600

utilities & telecommunications — 42,900

hotels & accommodation — 43,000

REAL ESTATE

California runs on real-estate development. The scale of building is huge and property values high. After the greatest real-estate bubble in history in the 2000s, the state suffered a devastating crash.

California has a massive inventory of buildings packed into cities and spread across the landscape, more than any other state. There are over 12 million housing units, of which over 7 million are single-family detached homes. Total office space is over 1 billion square feet.

California real estate is the priciest in the continental United States. The median home in 2010 cost just under $300,000, almost double the national average; the Bay Area median was twice the state average. The total value of California real estate in 2008 was $4.4 trillion.

California is home to some of the world's largest construction companies: KB Homes, Seeno, and Shapell Homes in housing, and Bechtel and Parsons in commercial/industrial. It has given rise to some of the largest realty firms, such as CB-Richard Ellis (Coldwell-Banker) and Cornish and Carey. California has long led the nation in large-scale construction projects, such as Boulder Dam, the Golden Gate Bridge, and the city of Lakewood.

Real-estate finance has been substantial since the 19th century, and Bank of America grew to be the nation's largest bank by 1930 through real-estate loans. Postwar California germinated the largest Savings and Loans in the country, such as American Savings. State mortgage lenders were key promoters of innovations such as the jumbo certificate of deposit and subprime loans, which ballooned the market in the 1980s and 2000s. At the peak of the housing bubble in 2006, almost a third of all mortgage loans in the country were issued in California.

Property development and lending are highly cyclical, more so than the economy at large. California has enjoyed major building booms every 20 years since the 1860s. At the peak of the boom of the 2000s, 150,000 new housing units went up every year, and almost a million people were working in construction, sales, and finance. But prices inflated beyond the reach of most people, leading to severe over-indebtedness. The bubble burst and California suffered the largest number of foreclosures and underwater mortgages, and the greatest dip in home values of any state, by far.

THE NATION'S PRICIEST HOUSES
Average price of detached
single-family home
in selected metropolitan areas
2005 & 2010

2005   2010

San Jose, CA
$744,500 $602,400

San Francisco, CA
$715,700 $525,300

San Diego, CA
$604,300 $385,200

Los Angeles, CA
$529,000 $316,700

New York, NY
$445,200 $393,700

Washington DC
$425,800 $325,300

Miami, FL
$363,900 $210,900

Chicago, IL
$264,200 $191,400

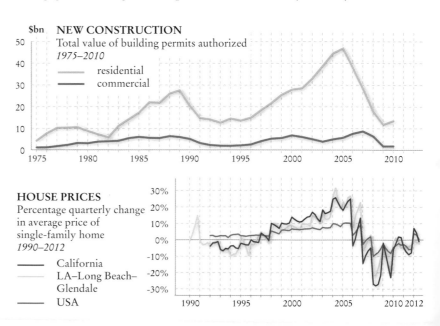

$bn   NEW CONSTRUCTION
Total value of building permits authorized
1975–2010
— residential
— commercial

HOUSE PRICES
Percentage quarterly change
in average price of
single-family home
1990–2012
— California
— LA–Long Beach–Glendale
— USA

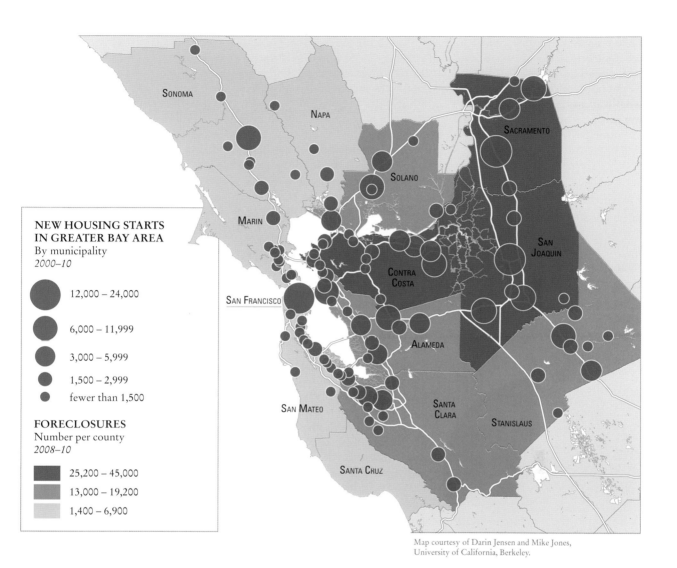

Map courtesy of Darin Jensen and Mike Jones,
University of California, Berkeley.

**NEW HOUSING STARTS
IN GREATER BAY AREA**
By municipality
2000–10

- 12,000 – 24,000
- 6,000 – 11,999
- 3,000 – 5,999
- 1,500 – 2,999
- fewer than 1,500

FORECLOSURES
Number per county
2008–10

- 25,200 – 45,000
- 13,000 – 19,200
- 1,400 – 6,900

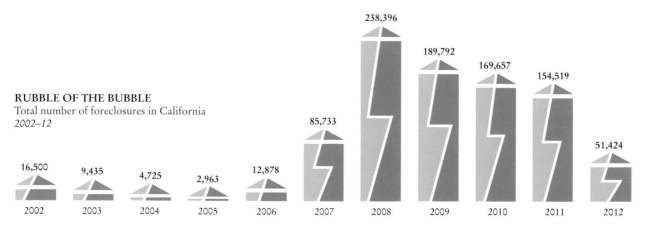

RUBBLE OF THE BUBBLE
Total number of foreclosures in California
2002–12

2002	2003	2004	2005	2006	2007	2008	2009	2010	2011	2012
16,500	9,435	4,725	2,963	12,878	85,733	238,396	189,792	169,657	154,519	51,424

HIGHWAYS & TRANSPORTATION

California has one of the most advanced transportation systems in the world, including highways, airports, seaports, and railroads. The challenges of city commuting are great, as are those of handling an immense flow of goods, within and beyond state borders.

California was a pioneer of modern highways and almost all are public. It is laced by one of the world's great networks, with more than 385,600 miles of roads. There are about 18 million registered vehicles, double the number in Texas or New York, and Californians drive over 332 billion miles a year.

Flows of commuter traffic in California's cities are enormous. Greater Los Angeles and the Bay Area have some of the worst congestion and longest commute times in the USA, especially from inland areas. But not all commuting is by car. Los Angeles County Metro runs the second largest bus system in the country by ridership, complemented by a fast-growing subway and light rail network.

The SF–Oakland metro area is second in the country in share of commuters using public transportation, after New York. The Bay Area is served by Bay Area Rapid Transit (BART) and four large bus systems. San Jose and San Francisco have light rail, and regional railroad and ferry commuting are making a comeback.

California is the main port of entry for Pacific sea trade. San Francisco was the biggest west coast port until 1950. The port complex of Los Angeles and Long Beach is now by far the largest in the United States and eighth in the world in 2011, in terms of volume of trade. Goods flow to and from the rest of the country by rail and truck, and through a huge warehouse complex in Riverside County. Oakland ranks fifth among US container ports.

California depends on air travel for both passengers and high-value freight such as electronics. The state has been a pioneer in aircraft, airports, and aviation. Today, the Bay Area has three major airports, Greater LA four. LAX is the busiest passenger terminal in the country and SFO is fifth. For years, the LA–SF corridor had more air traffic than any in the world. The metro areas as a whole rank seventh and thirteenth in the world in terms of passenger numbers.

With so much intra-state traffic, California is building a high-speed train linking northern and southern cities, running down the Central Valley and through the Tehachapi mountains. It is the largest public works project in the country at $69 billion (and rising) and is highly controversial.

MODE OF TRAVEL
By commuters
2009

- driving alone
- carpooling
- public transit
- biking
- walking
- other

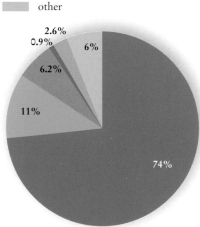

2.6%
0.9%
6%
6.2%
11%
74%

Los Angeles MSA
total workers: 5,806,655

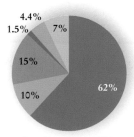

4.4%
1.5%
7%
15%
10%
62%

San Francisco MSA
total workers: 2,083,775

BAY AREA COMMUTER FLOWS
Number of daily journeys made between counties for the purposes of work
2010 projected

➡ 100,000 or more

➡ 50,000 – 99,999

➡ 10,000 – 49,999

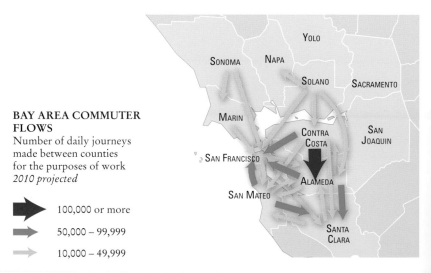

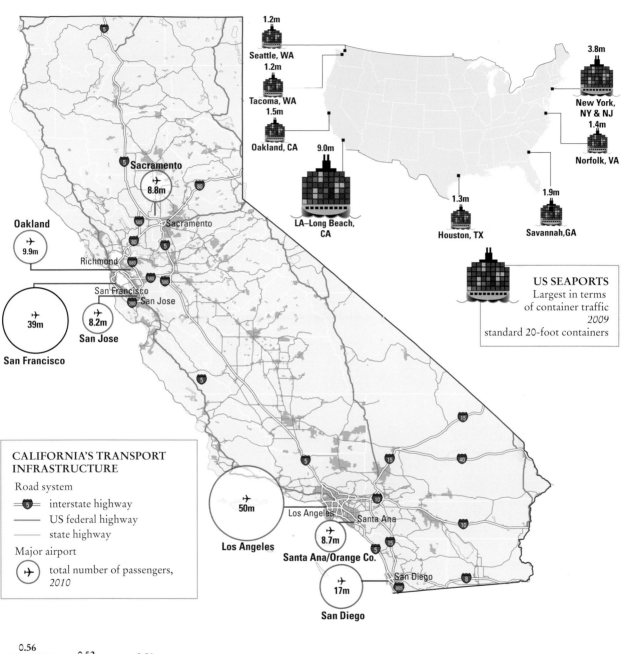

1.2m
Seattle, WA

1.2m
Tacoma, WA

1.5m
Oakland, CA

9.0m
LA–Long Beach, CA

3.8m
New York, NY & NJ

1.4m
Norfolk, VA

1.3m
Houston, TX

1.9m
Savannah, GA

US SEAPORTS
Largest in terms
of container traffic
2009
standard 20-foot containers

Sacramento
8.8m

Oakland
9.9m

San Francisco
39m

San Jose
8.2m

**CALIFORNIA'S TRANSPORT
INFRASTRUCTURE**

Road system

interstate highway

US federal highway

state highway

Major airport

total number of passengers,
2010

Los Angeles
50m

Santa Ana/Orange Co.
8.7m

San Diego
17m

0.56
Connecticut,
Iowa

0.52
North
Dakota

0.51
Michigan

0.49
South
Dakota

0.48
California

0.42
US average

**AUTOMOBILES
PER CAPITA**
Highest states
compared with average
2010

65

Chapter Five

WATER & ENERGY

Water and energy are the lifeblood of modern society. Since California is one of the great centers of thirsty agribusiness, water policy is often more critical than energy policy. As Californians are wont to say: "Whiskey is for drinking, water is for fighting over." Not to be outdone, California's 2001 energy crisis ended in the recall of a governor and the fall of mighty Enron, the world's largest energy trader.

Water supply is always a balancing act in California. The state's climate knows no "normal" year; averages include many years of drought and many of ample precipitation. The state's many dams, lengthy canals and deep wells work to smooth out the supply, but nothing is ever certain.

Water allocation is even trickier, with too many competing users. Agriculture still takes the lion's share of water, but California's cities are growing fast, and they pose a direct challenge to farming's historic dominance. Not that urban users are more virtuous: the majority of city water goes to irrigating lawns and gardens, not to drinking. But cities can afford to pay many times more per gallon.

California's energy picture is at odds with most of the rest of the USA, as well. Heating and electricity generation come less from coal than from natural gas. Oil is mostly used to fuel California's immense transportation system. The state was an early leader in hydro-electricity generation and use, but there is little further room for expansion. Nuclear energy remains extremely controversial.

California's pattern of energy consumption is unique in the USA, too. The state has led the way in conservation policy since the 1970s, with per person use far below that of most states. Energy consumption is dominated by transportation, due to the size of the state, the number of cars in cities, and massive truck traffic. Water pumping is another major energy-eater; the pumps on the California aqueduct use as much as large cities. And the new desalination plant being built for San Diego will be a huge drain on energy.

State policy has encouraged renewable energy development—wind, geothermal, hydro, biomass, and solar—for decades, with a new push in the 2000s, especially in large solar and wind farms in desert areas. The main argument for energy conservation and alternatives is climate change, but the lessons of California's energy crisis of a decade ago still haunt the state.

Solar panels
in Death Valley.

WATER SUPPLY

Northern California has abundant rainfall and the Sierra a large snowpack; excess runoff is stored and moved south to supply agriculture and cities in the southern half of the state.

California is surprisingly wet. The north lies within the climatic zone of the Pacific Northwest, the center has ample winter rain, and the Sierra Nevada receives a large snowfall. But the greatest water demand is in the summer and in the southern half of the state, requiring massive storage dams and lengthy aqueducts. California has a highly variable climate, with wide swings in precipitation from year to year and long periods of drought. This requires even larger storage facilities and water exports.

Roughly 30 million acre-feet (MAF) are diverted through this vast water infrastructure. The majority is supplied from local dams and canals, but the largest sources are the federal Central Valley Project and State Water Project, which pump an average of 5 MAF south from the Sacramento–San Joaquin Delta to serve San Joaquin Valley agriculture and the cities of Southern California. The Colorado River supplies another 4.4 MAF to the latter and the Imperial Valley.

This massive engineering of rivers has its costs. Diversion of freshwater flows into the San Francisco Bay and Delta has caused significant declines in fish and wildlife. There has been a push-back to reserve water for environmental uses, such as releases during salmon runs, minimum summer flows, wetlands restoration, and groundwater recharge. Environmental water use is estimated to increase modestly to between 0.5 and 1.0 MAF per year over the next two decades.

The total storage capacity of California's groundwater basins is estimated to be 1 billion acre-feet, but the usable storage is only one-quarter of that. Only a certain amount of water can be extracted regularly without seriously depleting the aquifers. Groundwater overdraft, which occurs when more water is removed than is recharged, is currently estimated to be 1.5 MAF per year.

California's enormous storage and transfer system is one of the largest water works in the world. Yet it is under tremendous pressure from the risk of catastrophic floods and levee breaks, erosion by higher sea levels, a smaller snowpack due to global warming, and rising pumping costs from higher energy prices.

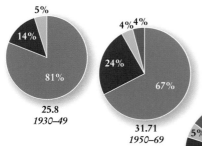

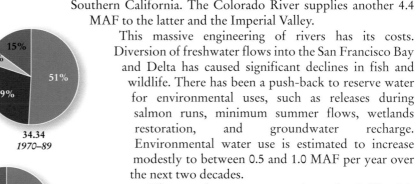

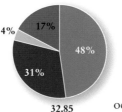

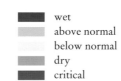

OUTFLOW AND USE
Average annual outflow of Sacramento and San Joaquin rivers at the Delta and breakdown of use
1930–2005
million acre-feet

- outflow to ocean
- diversions and use before reaching Delta
- in-Delta use
- exports

FLUCTUATION BETWEEN WET AND DRY YEARS
Classification of year based on index derived from unimpaired water runoff
1901–2012

- wet
- above normal
- below normal
- dry
- critical

Sacramento Valley

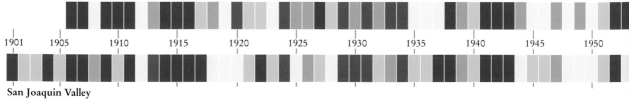

San Joaquin Valley

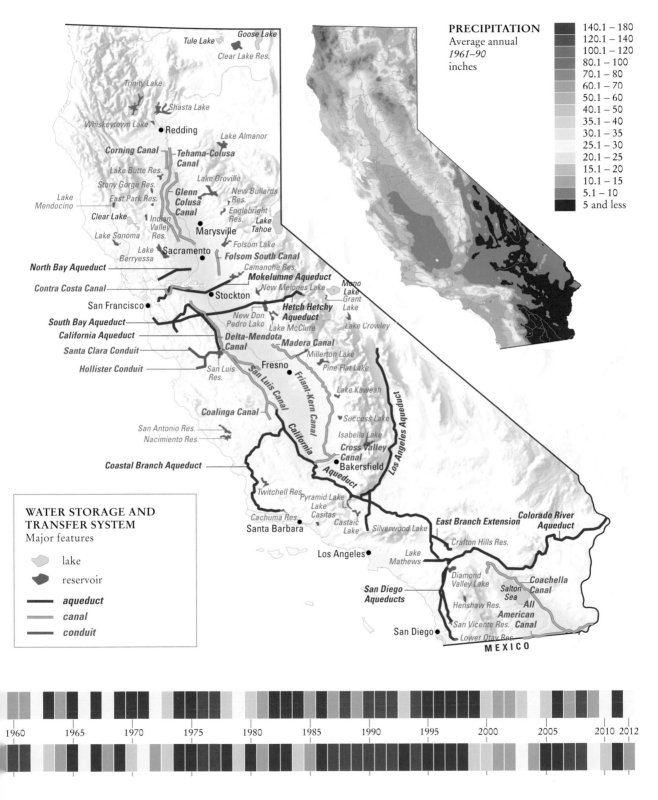

PRECIPITATION
Average annual
1961–90
inches

	140.1 – 180
	120.1 – 140
	100.1 – 120
	80.1 – 100
	70.1 – 80
	60.1 – 70
	50.1 – 60
	40.1 – 50
	35.1 – 40
	30.1 – 35
	25.1 – 30
	20.1 – 25
	15.1 – 20
	10.1 – 15
	5.1 – 10
	5 and less

Tule Lake
Goose Lake
Clear Lake Res.
Trinity Lake
Shasta Lake
Whiskeytown Lake
Redding
Lake Almanor
Corning Canal
Tehama-Colusa Canal
Lake Butte Res.
Stony Gorge Res.
Lake Oroville
East Park Res.
New Bullards Res.
Lake Mendocino
Glenn Colusa Canal
Englebright Res.
Clear Lake
Indian Valley Res.
Lake Tahoe
Lake Sonoma
Marysville
Folsom Lake
Lake Berryessa
Sacramento
Folsom South Canal
Camanche Res.
North Bay Aqueduct
Mokelumne Aqueduct
Mono Lake
Contra Costa Canal
New Melones Lake
Grant Lake
Stockton
San Francisco
Hetch Hetchy Aqueduct
South Bay Aqueduct
New Don Pedro Lake
Lake Crowley
California Aqueduct
Lake McClure
Delta-Mendota Canal
Santa Clara Conduit
Madera Canal
Millerton Lake
Hollister Conduit
Pine Flat Lake
San Luis Res.
Fresno
San Luis Canal
Friant-Kern Canal
Lake Kaweah
Coalinga Canal
Los Angeles Aqueduct
San Antonio Res.
Success Lake
Nacimiento Res.
Isabella Lake
Cross Valley Canal
Coastal Branch Aqueduct
Bakersfield
California Aqueduct
Twitchell Res.
Pyramid Lake
East Branch Extension
Colorado River Aqueduct
Lake Casitas
Cachuma Res.
Castaic Lake
Silverwood Lake
Santa Barbara
Crafton Hills Res.
Los Angeles
Lake Mathews
Diamond Valley Lake
Coachella Canal
San Diego Aqueducts
Salton Sea
Henshaw Res.
All American Canal
San Diego
San Vicente Res.
Lower Otay Res.
MEXICO

WATER STORAGE AND TRANSFER SYSTEM
Major features

- lake
- reservoir
- *aqueduct*
- *canal*
- *conduit*

1960 1965 1970 1975 1980 1985 1990 1995 2000 2005 2010 2012

WATER USE

Water use exceeds natural supply in many parts of California, especially in drought years. Water conservation has checked the growth of consumption, and it must continue.

Agriculture uses the lion's share of water in California, mostly in the Central Valley and Imperial Valley, but growth of the cities has driven urban water use upward as a proportion of the total. Even as cities eat away at nearby farmland, agricultural output and intensification continue to climb. Despite California's growth, water conservation has taken some of the sting out of the rise of water demand.

Agricultural water use has been declining due to better monitoring of soil moisture, plant stress, and weather, and a shift in land-use from cropland to grazing and wildlife habitat. Cropping patterns are sensitive to water and energy (pumping) prices, and growers are gradually shifting production away from low-value, water-intensive crops. Nevertheless, there are barriers to more rational water use, such as long-term water rights and contracts, federal crop subsidies, and demand for livestock feed. Estimates for agricultural water use project a modest reduction over the next two decades.

The urban share of water use has steadily increased from 10 percent in the 1960s to roughly 25 percent today. At the same time, water conservation practices and demand management (metering and pricing) have sufficiently reduced per capita use that total urban water demand has remained roughly constant for more than a decade. With population growth, however, total urban water consumption is projected to rise by between 15 and 25 percent from current levels over the next two decades. Significantly, nearly half of urban water goes to landscaping—in other words, to plants not people.

Groundwater overdraft is a major concern in central and southern California, where local water supplies, supplemented by sizable water imports, are insufficient to meet the requirements of residents, growers, and businesses. Environmentalists have called for water conservation to protect aquifers, and fewer exports to protect rivers and wildlife, but environmental water use is not expected to rise markedly, given competing demands.

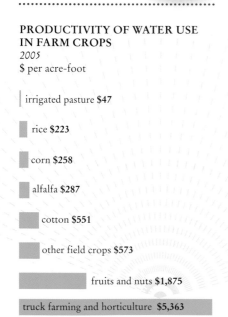

WATER USE
2005

agricultural 75%

urban 25%

energy 2%

industrial 6%

commercial 13%

large landscape 10%

residential interior 32%

residential landscape 37%

PRODUCTIVITY OF WATER USE IN FARM CROPS
2005
$ per acre-foot

irrigated pasture **$47**

rice **$223**

corn **$258**

alfalfa **$287**

cotton **$551**

other field crops **$573**

fruits and nuts **$1,875**

truck farming and horticulture **$5,363**

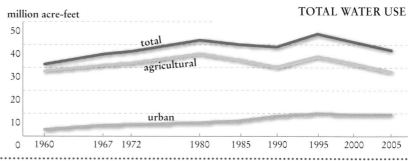

TOTAL WATER USE

million acre-feet

total

agricultural

urban

1960 · 1967 · 1972 · 1980 · 1985 · 1990 · 1995 · 2000 · 2005

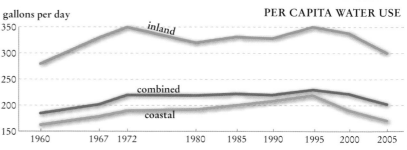

PER CAPITA WATER USE

gallons per day

inland

combined

coastal

1960 · 1967 · 1972 · 1980 · 1985 · 1990 · 1995 · 2000 · 2005

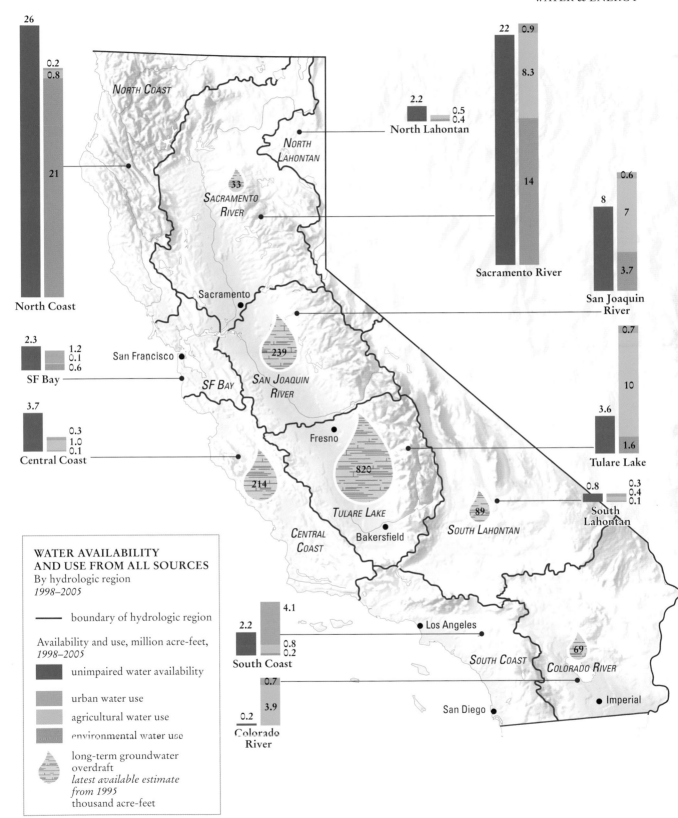

26

0.2
0.8

21

North Coast

22 | 0.9
8.3
14

Sacramento River

2.2 | 0.5
0.4
North Lahontan

8 | 0.6
7
3.7
San Joaquin River

NORTH COAST

NORTH LAHONTAN

SACRAMENTO RIVER

33

Sacramento

2.3 | 1.2
0.1
0.6
SF Bay

San Francisco

3.7 | 0.3
1.0
0.1
Central Coast

239

SAN JOAQUIN RIVER

SF BAY

Fresno

0.7
10
3.6 | 1.6
Tulare Lake

820

214

TULARE LAKE

CENTRAL COAST

Bakersfield

89

SOUTH LAHONTAN

0.8 | 0.3
0.4
0.1
South Lahontan

**WATER AVAILABILITY
AND USE FROM ALL SOURCES**
By hydrologic region
1998–2005

——— boundary of hydrologic region

Availability and use, million acre-feet,
1998–2005

▇ unimpaired water availability

▇ urban water use

▇ agricultural water use

▇ environmental water use

💧 long-term groundwater
overdraft
*latest available estimate
from 1995*
thousand acre-feet

2.2 | 4.1
0.8
0.2
South Coast

Los Angeles

SOUTH COAST

69

COLORADO RIVER

0.7
3.9
0.2
Colorado River

San Diego

Imperial

71

ENERGY: FOSSIL FUELS

California has one of the lowest rates of energy consumption in the United States. Fossil fuels, mostly foreign and domestic imports, dominate energy supply, despite efforts to develop alternative sources.

Adequate, reliable, and affordable energy is essential for modern economies and human well-being. California's total energy demand is second only to that of Texas, thanks to its large population and leadership in energy-intensive industries (chemical, forest, glass, electronics, and petroleum). Yet its mild climate, high energy prices, and consumer activism, coupled with technological advances in energy efficiency, have contributed towards a moderate but steady decline in per capita energy consumption. This is one of the lowest per capita rates in the country, about 30 percent below the US average, although in the global context it is above that of most European countries and more than three times the world average.

Transportation accounts for over half of California's energy consumption. Residential and commercial use—primarily for the heating and cooling of buildings—account for nearly a third.

Fossil fuels provide about 80 percent of California's energy supply, as in the US as a whole. Coal is used less in California, compared to the US, due to lack of nearby sources and strict emission laws. The state is one of the top producers of crude oil in the country, accounting for more than 10 percent of US production. Most production takes place in the Los Angeles basin, Kern county, and offshore Southern California. But a steady decline of local output over the last two decades has led to almost 60 percent of oil being imported. Natural gas is the other main energy source, with 90 percent of it drawn from out-of-state sources.

More than a third of primary energy supply is used up in generating electricity, refining petroleum products, and distribution losses. Of California's remaining energy use, oil accounts for three-fifths, and almost 90 percent of that is used for transportation. Natural gas accounts for less than one-fifth, mostly for space heating. The remainder of energy used is in the form of electricity from gas, coal, hydro, nuclear, and renewables.

California energy policy has led the nation, thanks to a strong environmental movement and technically innovative industries. A host of energy-saving rules were adopted in the wake of the energy crisis of the 1970s, which has contributed to lowering energy consumption. Reducing greenhouse gas emissions became a priority in the 2000s. A bill signed in 2011 set a goal for 2020 of 33 percent of the state's electricity retail sales to be generated by renewables.

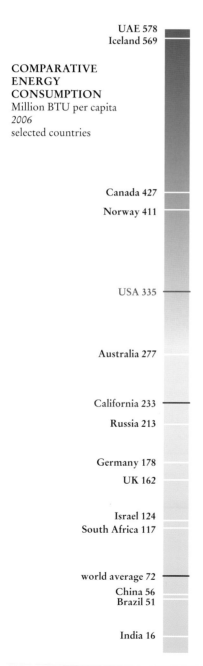

COMPARATIVE ENERGY CONSUMPTION
Million BTU per capita
2006
selected countries

UAE 578
Iceland 569
Canada 427
Norway 411
USA 335
Australia 277
California 233
Russia 213
Germany 178
UK 162
Israel 124
South Africa 117
world average 72
China 56
Brazil 51
India 16

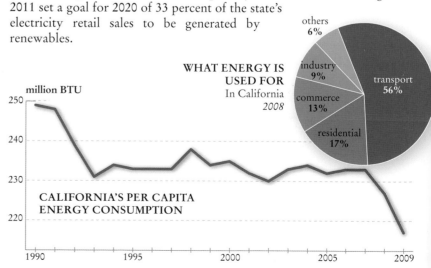

WHAT ENERGY IS USED FOR
In California
2008

others 6%
industry 9%
commerce 13%
residential 17%
transport 56%

million BTU

250
240
230
220

CALIFORNIA'S PER CAPITA ENERGY CONSUMPTION

1990   1995   2000   2005   2009

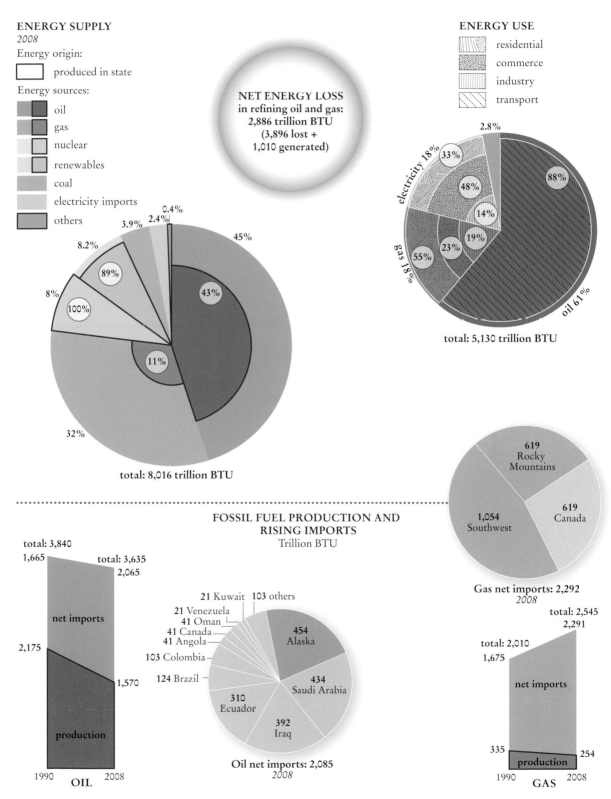

ENERGY SUPPLY
2008

Energy origin:

☐ produced in state

Energy sources:

▨ oil
▨ gas
☐ nuclear
☐ renewables
▨ coal
▨ electricity imports
▨ others

NET ENERGY LOSS
in refining oil and gas:
2,886 trillion BTU
(3,896 lost +
1,010 generated)

ENERGY USE

▤ residential
▦ commerce
▥ industry
▨ transport

2.8%

electricity 18% — 33%

88%

48%

14%

gas 18% — 55%

23% 19%

oil 61%

total: 5,130 trillion BTU

0.4%

3.9%

2.4%

8.2%

89%

8%

100%

45%

43%

11%

32%

total: 8,016 trillion BTU

619
Rocky
Mountains

1,054
Southwest

619
Canada

Gas net imports: 2,292
2008

FOSSIL FUEL PRODUCTION AND
RISING IMPORTS
Trillion BTU

total: 3,840
1,665

total: 3,635
2,065

net imports

2,175

1,570

production

1990 | OIL | 2008

21 Kuwait | 103 others
21 Venezuela
41 Oman
41 Canada
41 Angola
103 Colombia
124 Brazil

454
Alaska

434
Saudi Arabia

310
Ecuador

392
Iraq

Oil net imports: 2,085
2008

total: 2,545
2,291

total: 2,010
1,675

net imports

335

254

production

1990 | GAS | 2008

73

ENERGY: ELECTRICITY

Total electricity demand has been rising in California due to overall growth plus inland migration. Yet higher prices, government policies, and technical change have kept per capita electricity consumption flat over the last two decades.

California is the largest consumer of electricity in the nation after Texas. Demand has been growing at a steady rate of 1.25 percent annually, while peak demand has risen more rapidly (1.35%) due to urban growth in hotter inland areas. Nonetheless, average per capita electricity use has remained flat, hovering around 7,000 kWh per capita, almost 40 percent lower than the national average.

Electricity is the most versatile of energy sources and the one growing the fastest in the modern era of electronics. Yet most electricity is still used for heating and cooling of buildings and water. Larger homes, more lighting, and bigger appliances have fed the increase in electricity demand, along with computerization of business and industry (including massive server farms for the internet).

California has been able to contain per capita electricity consumption through a mix of cultural change and technological advances, such as efficient appliances, smarter thermostats, and better insulation. Energy conservation has been prompted by higher prices, consumer education, and energy policies such as lighting standards, building codes, and utility regulation.

Gas-fired power plants account for almost half of California's electric generation. Coal-fired plants are the second largest source, even though the state has no coal of its own. California's two nuclear power plants are next, followed by its many hydroelectric facilities. The state is one of the largest hydro-power producers, but is dependent on adequate rainfall to assure supply. California is a leader in renewables, such as geothermal and solar, but these still make up barely a tenth of total supply.

California is the largest importer of electricity from out-of-state sources, through the giant western states power grid. California's electricity system has been upgraded since the state suffered four major blackouts in 2000 and 2001. Peak demand due to economic boom and high temperatures collided with supply constrained by drought in the Northwest, a shortage of power plants, and a key bottleneck in transmission. Enron and other intermediaries then held back supply to create high prices, which cost the state billions of dollars in emergency contracts to keep power flowing.

California's aging power plants are in need of large capital investment to realize their potential to become 20 to 30 percent more efficient using current technologies and reduce greenhouse gas emissions. California's aging electricity distribution grid could also use modern technology to detect and respond to problems in real time.

PER CAPITA ELECTRICITY CONSUMPTION
2008

Imports		In-state production
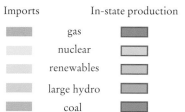	gas	
	nuclear	
	renewables	
	large hydro	
	coal	

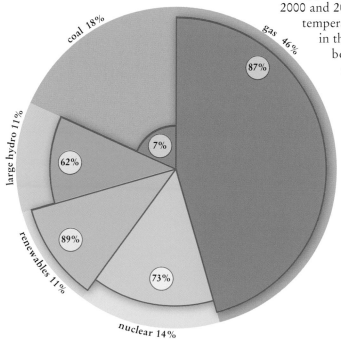

coal 18%

gas 46%

large hydro 11%

renewables 11%

nuclear 14%

87%

7%

62%

89%

73%

ELECTRICITY
CONSUMPTION
kWh per capita
2010

- 20,000 – 27, 457
- 15,000 – 19,999
- 10,000 – 14,999
- 6,721 – 9,999

Electricity prices
January 2011

below 7.5 cents/kWh

above 13.0 cents/kWh

ELECTRICITY CONSUMPTION TRENDS
1990–2010

California USA

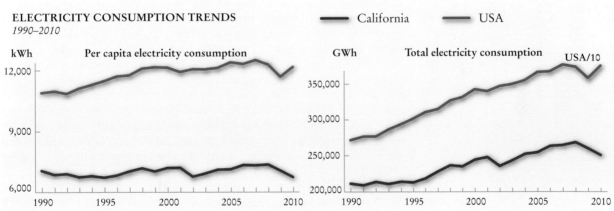

kWh   **Per capita electricity consumption**

GWh   **Total electricity consumption**

CHANGE IN ENERGY CONSUMPTION PER HOUSEHOLD
For selected uses
1990–2009

Decrease due to technology and policy

−44%	central air conditioning	*building codes on insulation and appliance standards*
−27%	refrigeration	*appliance efficiency*
−29%	space heating	*better insulation in buildings*
water heating **−2%**		*better technology but further advances required*

Increase due to consumption

desire for more lighting **lighting** **16%**

75

RENEWABLE ENERGY

California is a leading producer of renewable energy, but the goal of significantly increasing the share of electricity generated by renewables faces many obstacles.

Renewable sources—geothermal, wind, solar, biomass, and small hydro—account for 11.7 percent of in-state generation of California's total electricity sales. Large hydroelectric plants, which typically involve dams and reservoirs, generate a further 12.8 percent, but are not included in the California Renewable Portfolio Standards (RPS) accounts.

Geothermal energy is currently the largest contributor of renewable energy within the state, and California produces more than two-thirds of the US total. It is the second largest producer of wind energy, and both on-shore and off-shore wind power have been identified as having potential for future development. However, concerns about noise pollution, bird deaths, and risk of brush fires need to be addressed. Wave and tidal energy can also potentially be used for future renewable energy generation.

Biomass plants are distributed throughout California. Requirements for obtaining a permit include the ability to meet air-quality standards and the proper disposal of hazardous materials. Small hydro contributes the same share of the state's energy as biomass. The impact on river flow and wildlife, while less than large dams, needs to be evaluated before permits are issued.

Solar energy contributes only 3 percent of California's renewable energy and a tiny 0.4 percent of total electricity sales, but it holds the maximum promise for future development. Investors favor large installations in semi-arid areas, but these can have negative impacts on biodiversity and Native American sites. The state has provided incentives for installing solar panels on rooftops. Residential solar is increasingly cost competitive with utility rates, and utilities are required by law to buy electricity fed back to the grid at wholesale prices.

In order to increase energy independence and reduce greenhouse gas emissions, California has launched a series of initiatives over the last decade. In 2011, the state set the ambitious goal of renewable energy sources contributing 20 percent, 25 percent, and 33 percent of electricity sales by 2013, 2016, and 2020 respectively. New challenges are posed, however, by the need to meet environmental standards, develop new transmission infrastructure, and integrate large amounts of intermittent renewable energy.

CALIFORNIA TAKES THE LEAD
Comparison of California's renewable energy generation with that of two largest states in each category *2008* thousand kWh

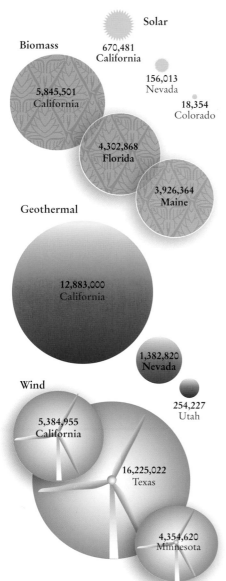

Solar

670,481
California

156,013
Nevada

18,354
Colorado

Biomass

5,845,501
California

4,302,868
Florida

3,926,364
Maine

Geothermal

12,883,000
California

1,382,820
Nevada

254,227
Utah

Wind

5,384,955
California

16,225,022
Texas

4,354,620
Minnesota

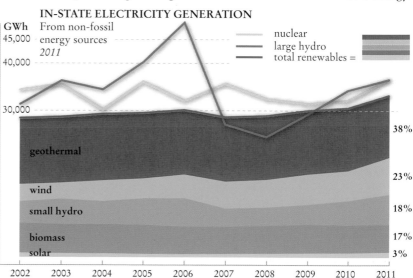

IN-STATE ELECTRICITY GENERATION

GWh — From non-fossil energy sources *2011*

nuclear
large hydro
total renewables =

45,000
40,000
30,000

geothermal — 38%
wind — 23%
small hydro — 18%
biomass — 17%
solar — 3%

2002 2003 2004 2005 2006 2007 2008 2009 2010 2011

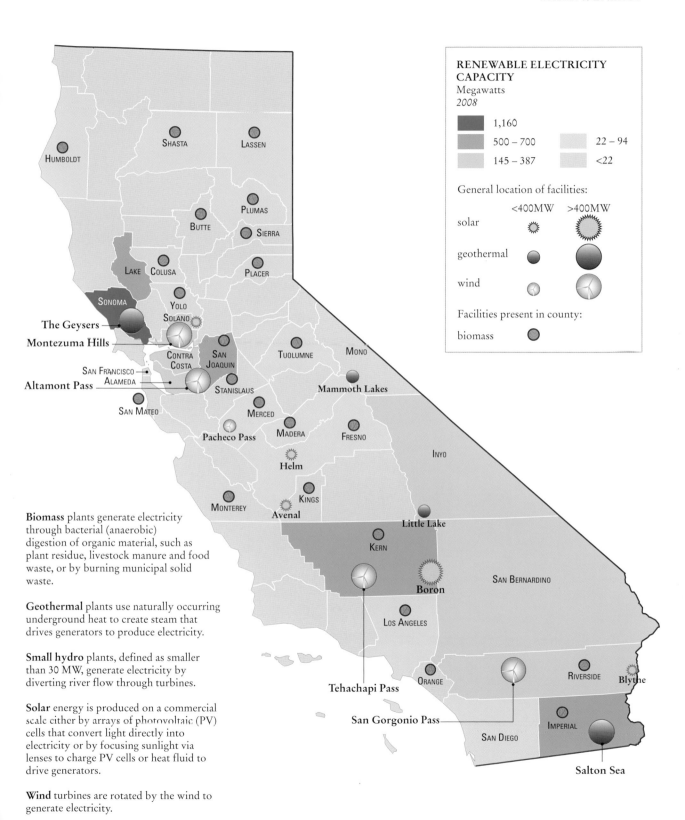

RENEWABLE ELECTRICITY CAPACITY
Megawatts
2008

1,160	
500 – 700	22 – 94
145 – 387	<22

General location of facilities:

	<400MW	>400MW
solar		
geothermal		
wind		

Facilities present in county:

biomass

Biomass plants generate electricity through bacterial (anaerobic) digestion of organic material, such as plant residue, livestock manure and food waste, or by burning municipal solid waste.

Geothermal plants use naturally occurring underground heat to create steam that drives generators to produce electricity.

Small hydro plants, defined as smaller than 30 MW, generate electricity by diverting river flow through turbines.

Solar energy is produced on a commercial scale either by arrays of photovoltaic (PV) cells that convert light directly into electricity or by focusing sunlight via lenses to charge PV cells or heat fluid to drive generators.

Wind turbines are rotated by the wind to generate electricity.

77

Chapter Six

ENVIRONMENT

Climate change is the greatest environmental threat facing the world today, and California has an important role to play in rising to the challenge. It is one of the largest carbon emitters on Earth, yet it has been at times a leader in launching new initiatives to reduce emissions and introduce new "green" technologies. Because of previous steps taken to lower energy use, Californians' per capita energy consumption and carbon emissions are the lowest in the USA, and in recent years its state government has been far ahead of the nation in climate policy.

Climate change poses several immediate threats to California's environment and well-being. Because the state lies astride zones of regular drought, it may well suffer longer dry spells, along with the rest of the southwestern USA. Warmer winters means the Sierra snowpack will likely diminish. Both of these will put greater stress on an already overcommitted water supply for both cities and farms across the state. With rising temperatures, wildlife is already on the move to higher ground, and California's extraordinary biodiversity is in danger from a shrinking habitat.

Air and water pollution remain a major concern for California, given their implications for public health and wildlife conservation. What we call "pollution" is no more than the end game of modern life: the leftovers of the things we make and use, the miles we drive, and the water we flush away. Californians have fought pollution valiantly ever since the discovery of auto-based smog in the 1940s, and the state has been the leader in air-quality control, as well as in many facets of water-quality improvement.

Not all emissions are created equal, however, and many are hazardous substances. The proliferation and residues of toxic chemicals remain a serious challenge for regulators and for the well-being of all Californians.

California's powerful environmental movement has redirected its focus to deal with climate change, energy conservation, and carbon emissions, along with protecting wildlife habitat and public health. Of particular concern today is the reshaping of cities. Given the political clout of conservationists, climate-change denial is not popular in this state. Moreover, business people here look forward to profiting from green technologies in energy, building, and vehicles. Still, there is a strong undercurrent of resistance from those wedded to old ways of farming, traveling, building, and consuming.

Fish die-off from algal bloom in the Salton Sea, 2009. Rising salt, nutrient, and pesticide levels are making the lake less and less habitable.

CLIMATE CHANGE

Global climate change is being felt in California in the form of rising average temperatures and sea level, weather extremes, and more wildfires. The implications for water supply, flooding, and ecosystems are potentially grave.

Climate change is critical for California. The West is heating up faster than any other region of the United States: warming by 1.7 degrees Fahrenheit between 2003 and 2007, 70 percent above the global average. California has experienced long-run increases in average temperatures, sea levels, and extreme weather events.

Higher summer temperatures demand more irrigation and cooling water. Warmer winters are likely to decrease snowpack in the Sierra Nevada and lead to earlier snowmelt, shortening the winter recreation season, reducing water storage for cities and irrigation, and altering stream flow that supports aquatic life. The number of winter chill hours has decreased since 1950, and if this trend were to continue it would impact the production of fruit, vine, and nut crops.

California is a land of periodic droughts, which may become more frequent with global warming. Greater climate variation means more heat waves, such as the one in 2006 that caused 140 deaths. The elderly and the poor are at a higher risk from such climatic extremes. Drought, heat, and strong winds increase the frequency of wildfires, which burned millions of acres and hundreds of suburban and recreation homes in an unprecedented decade of conflagration since 2000.

Ecosystems are sensitive to climate changes. The shift of ponderosa pine forest in Sierra Nevada east by more than 4.4 miles (7.1 km) and upwards by 637 ft (196 meters) between 1934 and 1996 has been attributed to rising temperatures. The waters of Lake Tahoe are warming at almost twice the rate of the oceans, modifying the lake's thermal structure and threatening its clarity. Endemic species that cannot shift their range will be the hardest hit by global warming.

During the past century, sea levels along California's coast have risen about 7 inches (178mm), and are predicted to rise by another 7 to 20 inches by the year 2100. This will impact low-lying and filled areas around San Francisco Bay and other estuaries. The danger is heightened during winter tidal surges, which can also lead to levee failures in the Delta and saltwater intrusion into coastal aquifers.

Human responsibility for climate change over the last 50 to 250 years, primarily by greenhouse gas emissions from fossil fuels, cattle, and forest clearance, is well established. California needs to stay a national leader in recognizing climate-change impacts and implementing energy and land conservation policies.

WINTER CHILL HOURS

Trend in the change in number of hours per year when temperature drops below 45°F
1950–2008

Decrease of:
- ● 20 – 40 hours per year
- ● 15 – 20
- ● 5 – 15
- ○ 0 – 5

Increase of:
- ● 0 – 10

inches

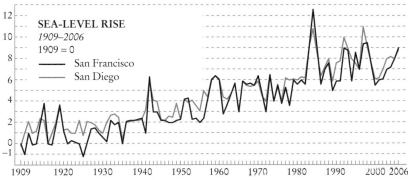

SEA-LEVEL RISE
1909–2006
1909 = 0
— San Francisco
— San Diego

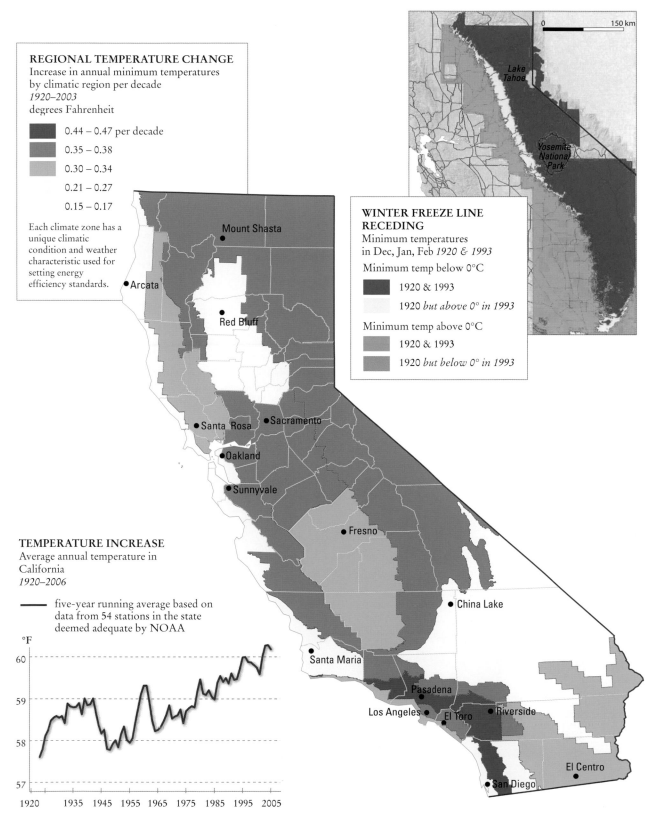

REGIONAL TEMPERATURE CHANGE
Increase in annual minimum temperatures
by climatic region per decade
1920–2003
degrees Fahrenheit

- 0.44 – 0.47 per decade
- 0.35 – 0.38
- 0.30 – 0.34
- 0.21 – 0.27
- 0.15 – 0.17

Each climate zone has a
unique climatic
condition and weather
characteristic used for
setting energy
efficiency standards.

0   150 km

**WINTER FREEZE LINE
RECEDING**
Minimum temperatures
in Dec, Jan, Feb *1920 & 1993*

Minimum temp below 0°C
- 1920 & 1993
- 1920 *but above 0° in 1993*

Minimum temp above 0°C
- 1920 & 1993
- 1920 *but below 0° in 1993*

TEMPERATURE INCREASE
Average annual temperature in
California
1920–2006

——— five-year running average based on
data from 54 stations in the state
deemed adequate by NOAA

°F
60
59
58
57

1920   1935   1945   1955   1965   1975   1985   1995   2005

81

CARBON EMISSIONS

California is a national leader in reducing carbon emissions through transportation planning, industrial controls, and the use of renewable energy, making it one of the lowest emitters per capita of greenhouse gases in the United States.

Because of its large economy, population, and area, California emits more greenhouse gases in total than all but about 18 countries, and more than any state except Texas, contributing roughly 1 percent of global emissions. From 1990 to 2008, California's total emissions increased by 11 percent, due to economic and population growth. Yet its per capita emissions declined by 7 percent. They are roughly 40 percent below the US average and behind that of most European nations.

The main sources of emissions are transportation (cars, trucks, trains, ships), industry (oil and gas refineries, manufacturing, construction, cement), electricity generation (power plants), and buildings (heating, cooling, and lighting).

The state took a major step to address climate change with the Global Warming Solutions Act of 2006 (administered by the Air Resources Board), which aims to reduce total greenhouse gas emissions to 1990 levels by the year 2020, and by much more in the years to follow, with a bold target of reducing per capita emissions sufficiently to put California on a par with India by 2050.

The 2006 Act relies on a number of measures, including the controversial cap-and-trade strategy to curtail emissions from the 600 largest point sources. Electric power plants, oil refineries, manufacturing, and other facilities must either reduce emissions or pay to make up the difference. Canada and several states are working together under the Western Climate Initiative to prevent displacement of pollution sources across borders to avoid regulations.

California has long been a leader in reducing vehicle emissions by means of new car standards, older vehicle tests, and low-carbon fuel standards, as well as transportation and urban planning. Vehicle emissions are most easily reduced by shifting to lighter vehicles, more efficient engines, and more compact cities, as well as greater use of mass transit. California has also led the way in energy-saving building codes and "green" building technologies.

COMPARATIVE EMISSIONS

Per capita emissions of carbon dioxide (CO_2) *2008*
metric tonnes

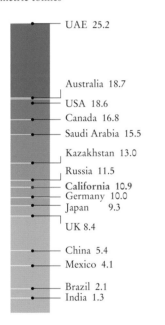

UAE 25.2

Australia 18.7
USA 18.6
Canada 16.8
Saudi Arabia 15.5
Kazakhstan 13.0
Russia 11.5
California 10.9
Germany 10.0
Japan 9.3
UK 8.4
China 5.4
Mexico 4.1
Brazil 2.1
India 1.3

TRENDS IN GHG EMISSIONS

Per capita emissions of all greenhouse gases
1990–2008 tonnes CO_2e

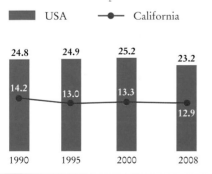

USA · California

	1990	1995	2000	2008
USA	24.8	24.9	25.2	23.2
California	14.2	13.0	13.3	12.9

VEHICLE MILES TRAVELED PER CAPITA

Selected states compared with US average
2006

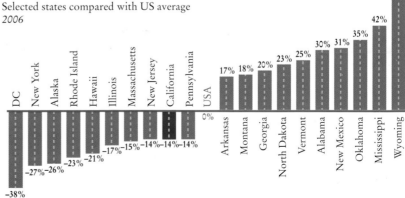

DC	New York	Alaska	Rhode Island	Hawaii	Illinois	Massachusetts	New Jersey	California	Pennsylvania	USA	Arkansas	Montana	Georgia	North Dakota	Vermont	Alabama	New Mexico	Oklahoma	Mississippi	Wyoming
−38%	−27%	−26%	−23%	−21%	−17%	−15%	−14%	−14%	−14%	0%	17%	18%	20%	23%	25%	30%	31%	35%	42%	82%

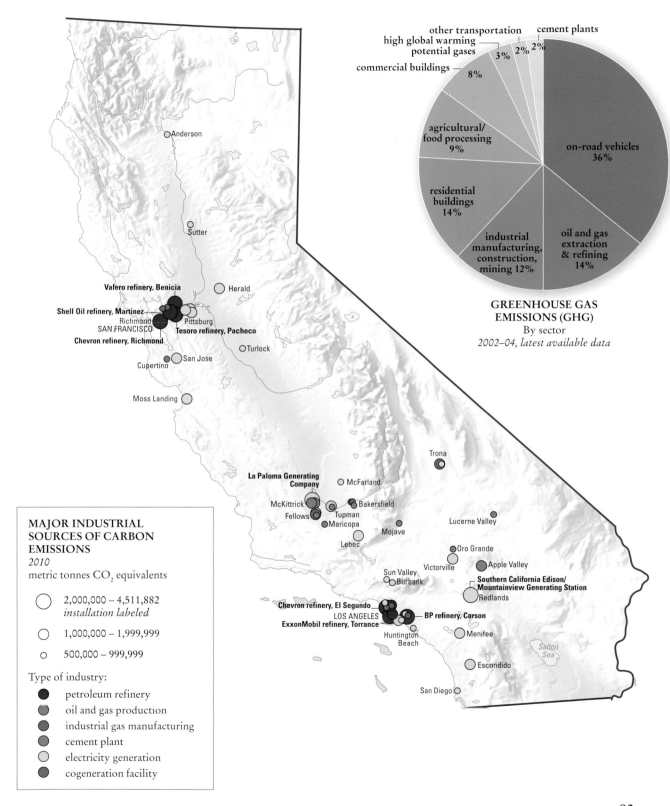

**GREENHOUSE GAS
EMISSIONS (GHG)**
By sector
2002–04, latest available data

Pie chart:
- on-road vehicles 36%
- oil and gas extraction & refining 14%
- industrial manufacturing, construction, mining 12%
- residential buildings 14%
- agricultural/food processing 9%
- commercial buildings 8%
- high global warming potential gases 3%
- other transportation 2%
- cement plants 2%

**MAJOR INDUSTRIAL
SOURCES OF CARBON
EMISSIONS**
2010
metric tonnes CO_2 equivalents

- 2,000,000 – 4,511,882 *installation labeled*
- 1,000,000 – 1,999,999
- 500,000 – 999,999

Type of industry:
- petroleum refinery
- oil and gas production
- industrial gas manufacturing
- cement plant
- electricity generation
- cogeneration facility

Map labels:
Anderson, Sutter, Herald, Valero refinery, Benicia, Shell Oil refinery, Martinez, Richmond, SAN FRANCISCO, Pittsburg, Tesoro refinery, Pacheco, Chevron refinery, Richmond, Cupertino, San Jose, Turlock, Moss Landing, Trona, La Paloma Generating Company, McFarland, McKittrick, Fellows, Tupman, Bakersfield, Maricopa, Mojave, Lucerne Valley, Lebec, Oro Grande, Victorville, Apple Valley, Sun Valley, Burbank, Southern California Edison/Mountainview Generating Station, Redlands, Chevron refinery, El Segundo, LOS ANGELES, BP refinery, Carson, ExxonMobil refinery, Torrance, Huntington Beach, Menifee, Escondido, Salton Sea, San Diego

AIR POLLUTION

Although California has made dramatic progress in reducing air pollution, a majority of the population continues to breathe air that poses significant health risks.

Ozone and small particles are the most widespread air pollutants in California. Others include carbon monoxide, oxides of nitrogen, and sulfur dioxide, as well as toxic metals (lead, mercury, arsenic) and hazardous hydrocarbons (benzene, toluene). When particulates and nitrogen oxides react with sunlight and moisture they form smog—a white haze in winter and brown in summer. Ozone is produced when nitrogen oxides and certain reactive organics come in contact with heat and sunlight.

Pollutants come from a range of sources: stationary (refineries, factories, chemical plants), mobile (cars, trucks, ships), household (paint, spray cans, fireplaces), and dispersed (agriculture, gas stations, construction sites). Episodic sources include dust storms and wild fires.

Air pollutants can be trapped by mountainous terrain like that surrounding Los Angeles or meteorological conditions such as stable high pressure or temperature inversions. Pollutants are dispersed by wind and rain. But they don't just go away: prevailing winds push Bay Area smog into the Central Valley and LA's bad air into the Inland Empire.

Air pollution poses a major health risk. Ozone is associated with lung inflammation and asthma. Small particles increase respiratory infections and cardiovascular failure, notably in areas of heavy diesel engine use. Conversely, a drop in particulates raised life expectancy in US cities by an average of 5 months from 1980 to 2000.

Of the 25 places with the worst ozone pollution in the United States, 12 cities and 18 counties are in California. As for the 25 with the highest particulates, 10 cities and 15 counties are here. The worst regions in the state are Los Angeles, the Inland Empire, and the San Joaquin Valley.

Since the 1940s, California has led the nation in regulating air pollution. There has been a significant reduction in ozone due to mobile sources in spite of greater population and vehicle miles traveled, but particulate levels have not fallen because of increased shipping traffic. More needs to be done in controlling emissions from ships, power plants, diesel trucks and automobiles.

IMPACT ON HEALTH
Percentage of population in
Los Angeles–Long Beach–Riverside
area at risk of respiratory diseases
due to air pollution
2009

emphysema
1.4%

pediatric asthma
1.7%

chronic bronchitis
3.1%

adult asthma
5.8%

diabetes
6.6%

cardiovascular disease
25.3%

Poverty combines with **respiratory disease** to increase the health risk due to air pollution of nearly **15%** of the area's population.

EMISSIONS TRENDS
Tons per day, annual average
1975–2010

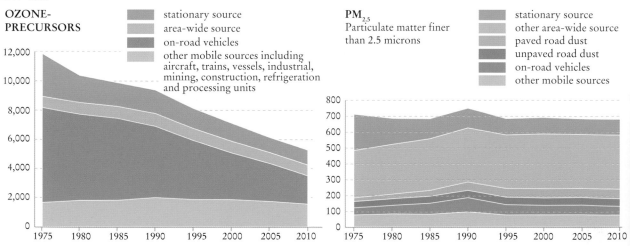

OZONE-PRECURSORS

- stationary source
- area-wide source
- on-road vehicles
- other mobile sources including aircraft, trains, vessels, industrial, mining, construction, refrigeration and processing units

PM$_{2.5}$
Particulate matter finer than 2.5 microns

- stationary source
- other area-wide source
- paved road dust
- unpaved road dust
- on-road vehicles
- other mobile sources

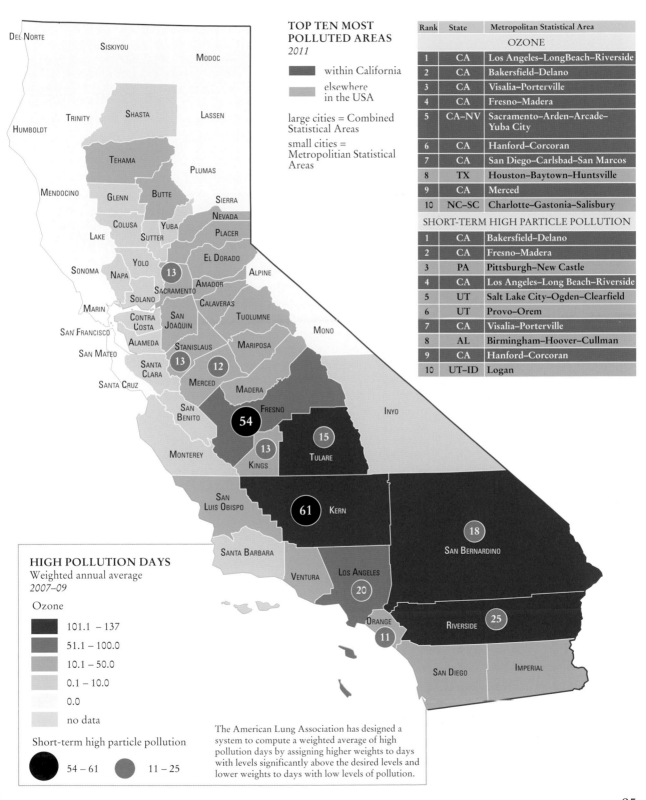

TOP TEN MOST POLLUTED AREAS
2011

■ within California

■ elsewhere in the USA

large cities = Combined Statistical Areas

small cities = Metropolitian Statistical Areas

Rank	State	Metropolitan Statistical Area
OZONE		
1	CA	Los Angeles–LongBeach–Riverside
2	CA	Bakersfield–Delano
3	CA	Visalia–Porterville
4	CA	Fresno–Madera
5	CA–NV	Sacramento–Arden–Arcade–Yuba City
6	CA	Hanford–Corcoran
7	CA	San Diego–Carlsbad–San Marcos
8	TX	Houston–Baytown–Huntsville
9	CA	Merced
10	NC–SC	Charlotte–Gastonia–Salisbury
SHORT-TERM HIGH PARTICLE POLLUTION		
1	CA	Bakersfield–Delano
2	CA	Fresno–Madera
3	PA	Pittsburgh–New Castle
4	CA	Los Angeles–Long Beach–Riverside
5	UT	Salt Lake City–Ogden–Clearfield
6	UT	Provo–Orem
7	CA	Visalia–Porterville
8	AL	Birmingham–Hoover–Cullman
9	CA	Hanford–Corcoran
10	UT–ID	Logan

HIGH POLLUTION DAYS
Weighted annual average
2007–09

Ozone

■ 101.1 – 137
■ 51.1 – 100.0
■ 10.1 – 50.0
■ 0.1 – 10.0
■ 0.0
■ no data

Short-term high particle pollution

● 54 – 61   ● 11 – 25

The American Lung Association has designed a system to compute a weighted average of high pollution days by assigning higher weights to days with levels significantly above the desired levels and lower weights to days with low levels of pollution.

WATER POLLUTION

California's surface, ground, and coastal waters suffer serious contamination from farms, cities, and industry, jeopardizing health, recreation, and wildlife. Toxic chemicals pose special risks to the public and the environment.

California has some of the most magnificent rivers, lakes, and coastal waters in the country, yet the EPA reported in 2011 that more than half of its 3 million acres of fresh water did not meet national water-quality standards and pollution had significantly increased in recent years. Lake Tahoe's famous clarity has declined by 25 percent over the last four decades.

Water must be of adequate quality for its intended use. Excesses of salinity and minerals reduce crop productivity. Contaminants from water runoff and high water temperatures resulting from dams and diversions harm fish, aquatic species, and birds. Heavy metals pose risks to the public and the environment.

Following the Clean Water Act of 1972, California made substantial progress on controlling "point sources" of pollutants, such as urban sewage and industrial waste. "Non-point sources" remain more difficult to control, in spite of the California Clean Water Act of 2006. Agricultural runoff contains sediment, nutrients from fertilizers and animal feed, and salts from irrigation. Urban runoff carries soil from construction sites, automobile oil and exhaust, garden fertilizers, pet wastes, overflow from faulty septic tanks, and trash from streets. Other major sources are recreational boating, ocean-going vessels, and poor forestry practices.

Runoff from the Coast Ranges contains high levels of arsenic, selenium, and mercury, among other metals, and mercury was dispersed widely during the mining era. California waters also suffer toxic contamination from refineries, automobiles, agricultural and garden pesticides, pharmaceuticals, personal-care products, and fire retardants. Under the Toxic Substances Control Act of 1976, EPA must prove, through intensive testing and cost–benefit analysis, that a chemical causes harm. As a result, EPA has declared only five chemicals harmful. By contrast, the European Union puts the burden of proof on the manufacturer.

Wildlife has been seriously affected by diseases carried in pet wastes, suffocation from trash, surface waters impaired by dams and diversions, and competition from exotic species. SF Bay is the most altered estuary in North America. Most of California's extensive wetlands, which nurture wildlife and filter pollutants, have been lost. Many native species declined dramatically during the last century.

Most coastal cities enjoy high-quality drinking water transported from the Sierra Nevada. But Central Valley drinking water from local rivers and groundwater is heavily contaminated by nitrates, pesticides, and heavy metals. The Federal and California Safe Drinking Water Acts of 1974 and 1976 have not been able to cope with all the threats, particularly those from new and untested chemicals.

SOURCES OF POLLUTION AND DISRUPTION BY HUMAN ACTIVITY

Percentage of surface water and rivers assessed as affected by each factor
2004

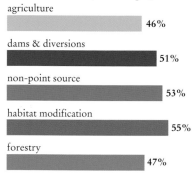

rivers and streams (15% sample)

- agriculture — 46%
- dams & diversions — 51%
- non-point source — 53%
- habitat modification — 55%
- forestry — 47%

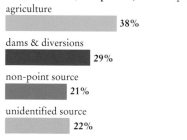

lakes, reservoirs, and ponds (50% sample)

- agriculture — 38%
- dams & diversions — 29%
- non-point source — 21%
- unidentified source — 22%

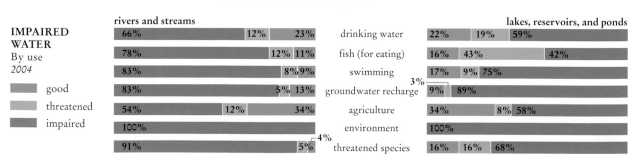

IMPAIRED WATER
By use
2004

- good
- threatened
- impaired

	rivers and streams				lakes, reservoirs, and ponds		
drinking water	66%	12%	23%		22%	19%	59%
fish (for eating)	78%	12%	11%		16%	43%	42%
swimming	83%		8% 9%		17%	9%	75%
groundwater recharge	83%	5%	13%		9%	3%	89%
agriculture	54%	12%	34%		34%	8%	58%
environment	100%				100%		
threatened species	91%	5%	4%		16%	16%	68%

Klamath River and major tributaries – *also* nutrients and dissolved oxygen.

NATIVE CALIFORNIAN FISH
Increase in number of endangered species
1989–2010

- reasonably secure
- special concern
- listed
- extinct

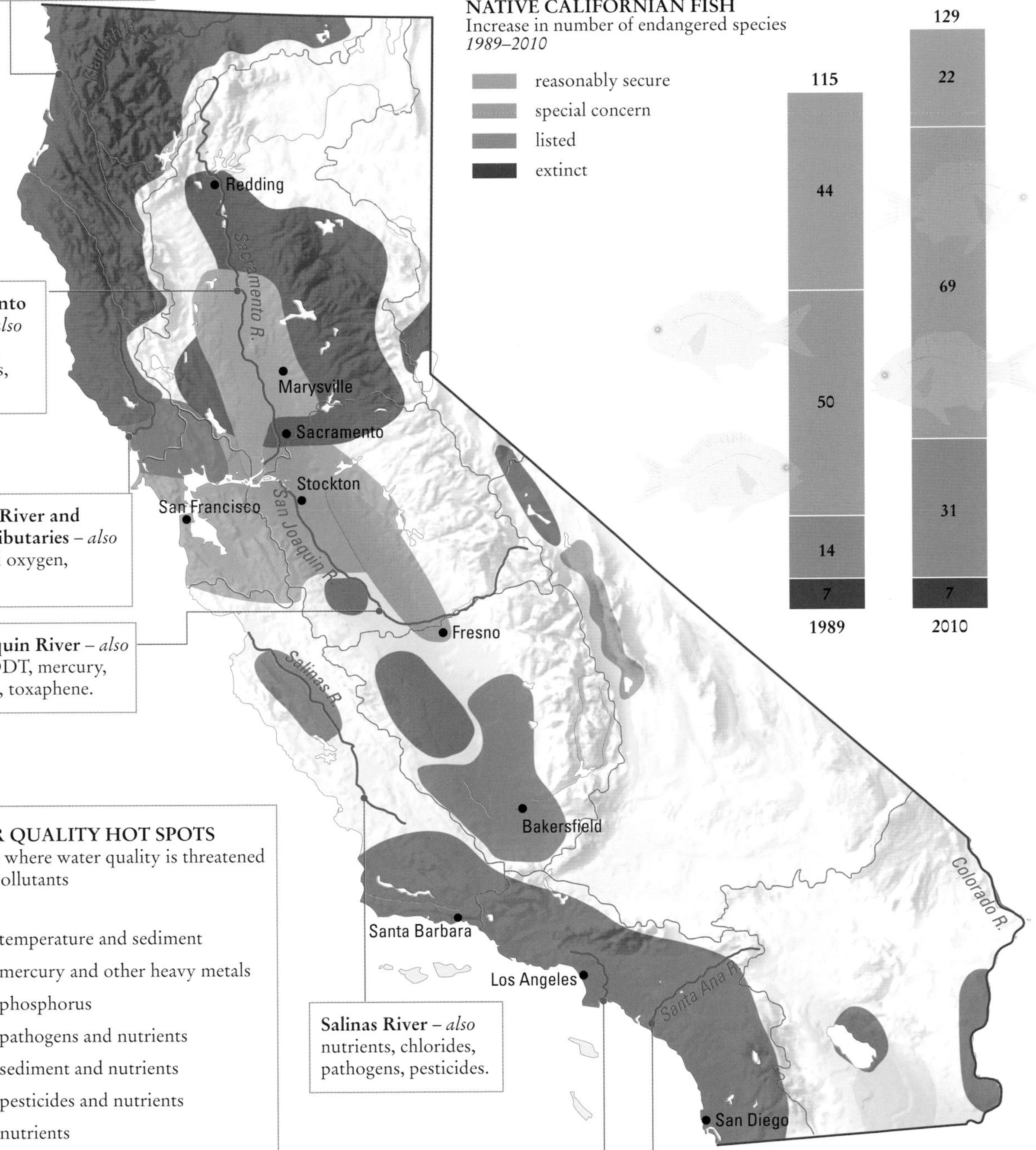

1989	2010
115	129
44	22
50	69
14	31
7	7

● Redding

Sacramento River – *also* fertilizer, pesticides, mercury.

Sacramento R.

● Marysville
● Sacramento
● Stockton

Russian River and major tributaries – *also* dissolved oxygen, mercury.

● San Francisco

San Joaquin R.

San Joaquin River – *also* boron, DDT, mercury, selenium, toxaphene.

● Fresno

Salinas R.

WATER QUALITY HOT SPOTS
Regions where water quality is threatened due to pollutants
2011

- temperature and sediment
- mercury and other heavy metals
- phosphorus
- pathogens and nutrients
- sediment and nutrients
- pesticides and nutrients
- nutrients
- metals and salts
- nitrates and pesticides
- pesticides
- pathogens, nutrients, and metals
- salts

● Bakersfield

Colorado R.

● Santa Barbara

Santa Ana R.

● Los Angeles

Salinas River – *also* nutrients, chlorides, pathogens, pesticides.

● San Diego

Los Angeles River – ammonia, cadmium, copper, lead, selenium, zinc.

Santa Ana River – *also* salinity, pathogens.

87

Chapter Seven

HEALTH & EDUCATION

If one is looking for markers of California's past glory and present crisis, health and education are good places to start. The state has been overwhelmed by a population surging toward 40 million. Whereas California rose to the challenge of postwar migration by building schools, hospitals, and college buildings by the thousands, it has failed its obligations to the latest influx of people. This can be attributed not only to budget shortages, but to a lack of political will reflecting the narrow concerns of the wealthy and White minority that still dominates California politics.

The health of Californians leaves much to be desired. It reflects, to a large degree, the inequalities of life conditions between different parts of the state and different classes and races. The well-to-do Bay Area is favored over the poorer and grittier interior valleys and mountain regions, and even over urban Southern California, home to the most immigrants and low-income workers.

The healthcare system is not helping to even out such disparities. California is among the worst in spending, and its healthcare ranks in the bottom third of the states. Health insurance is sorely lacking. To think that the country's first HMO, Kaiser-Permanente, was created in California in the 1940s! A hopeful sign is that California is among the leaders in seizing the opportunity to serve its uninsured under the ObamaCare program.

In the arena of public education, California has fallen far. Once among the top states in spending on K–12 schools, it is now among the bottom feeders. The performance of its children reflects this dismal record, with some of the worst test results and highest dropout rates in the country. California has sometimes been in the vanguard of efforts to improve pre-school opportunities, especially for children from poor and immigrant families. But the current funding squeeze hits here, too, and the great majority of children in need of pre-school programs are not enrolled.

Higher education was once the crown jewel of California, whose declared purpose was to allow all deserving students to have a chance at a college education. In the postwar era, California built up the country's greatest public system of higher education, in three tiers: community colleges, state colleges, and the University of California. All these were virtually free, until falling state revenues brought sharp tuition fee increases in the 2000s, as budgets were being slashed.

Surely, the most disconcerting aspect of the declining state of health and education in California is the way we are failing our children, and undermining the future of the state.

Berkeley students protest budget cuts and rising tuition fees at colleges and universities, 2009.

HEALTHCARE: QUALITY & OUTCOMES

Good health depends greatly on access to and quality of healthcare, on health behaviors, socio-economic conditions, and physical environment, which vary widely across California and create persistent disparities between places and racial/ethnic groups.

HEALTH DISPARITIES
In California
2000–01

Infant mortality: deaths per 1,000 births

 Blacks **12.7**

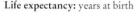 all **5.4**

Life expectancy: years at birth

Blacks

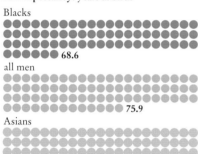 **68.6**

all men

75.9

Asians

80.4

Obesity incidence among men

Blacks
28%

Hispanics
28%

Whites
21%

Asians
7%

Good health depends upon a variety of factors, including personal behaviors (smoking, diet, exercise, drinking), socio-economic conditions (employment, income, education, support, safety), and physical environment (air and water quality, toxic exposure, playgrounds). Also important is access to and quality of clinical care.

Heart, cancer, stroke, and respiratory diseases are the major causes of mortality amongst Californians and Americans in general. Obesity, diabetes, and chronic health problems are major concerns that affect morbidity (including low birth-weight), as well as life expectancy. The incidence of such conditions varies strongly by racial/ethnic groups and social classes. High income, well-educated people enjoy better health than lower income, less-educated families, and Whites and Asians enjoy better health than Blacks and Hispanics, on average. For example, California's African Americans have a lower life expectancy than other groups, and higher rates of HIV and homicides. They also suffer more than double the incidence of infant mortality. Life expectancy of Hispanics, by contrast, is higher than the state average, but kept down by a high incidence of liver disease and diabetes. Both Hispanics and African-Americans have much higher rates of obesity than the state average, and Hispanic males have a higher incidence of drinking. In contrast, Asians have higher life expectancy, lower obesity, and less alcohol consumption than the average.

The quality of healthcare in California is a persistent concern. As reported by the US Agency for Healthcare Research and Quality, the state ranks 36th on a broad set of measures. Measurements of health and the quality of healthcare are difficult, but growing interest in personal "wellness" (a term invented in California) and the healthcare marketplace are driving efforts to improve data collection and reporting.

HEALTHCARE QUALITY
Range and setting of care and preventive services
2011

60.0 or more

50.0 – 59.9

40.0 – 49.9

less than 40.0

Assessment based on:

type of care: acute, chronic, and preventive
setting of care: hospital, ambulatory, nursing centers, and home
clinical targets: cancer, diabetes, heart and respiratory disease, maternal and child health
patient care: safety, timeliness, and personal concern.

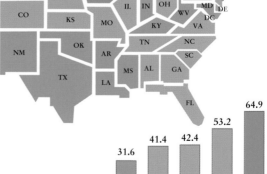

Comparison of selected states

TX	CA	NY	NJ	MA
31.6	41.4	42.4	53.2	64.9

The disparities in health between California's ethnic/racial communities suggest that good health is not simply a matter of personal habits but is tied to community-wide conditions such as wages, maternal care, drug and alcohol use, and diet. This is borne out by a comparison of average health experienced county by county. The coastal counties enjoy the best overall health, and the mountain counties in the north and San Joaquin Valley counties the worst. When it comes to factors influencing health, the coastal communities come out on top, with higher incomes, better diet, and better care, while most of the Central Valley counties are burdened with factors contributing to poor health, such as higher unemployment, lower wages, more drinking, worse air pollution.

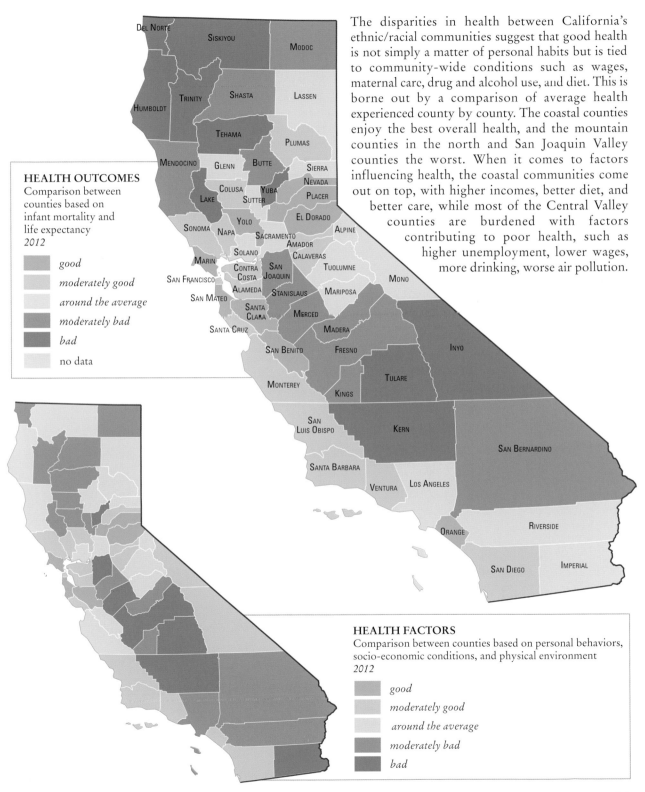

HEALTH OUTCOMES
Comparison between counties based on infant mortality and life expectancy
2012

good
moderately good
around the average
moderately bad
bad
no data

HEALTH FACTORS
Comparison between counties based on personal behaviors, socio-economic conditions, and physical environment
2012

good
moderately good
around the average
moderately bad
bad

91

Healthcare: Cost & Access

Healthcare costs have been rising rapidly, burdening families, employers, and governments. Yet California ranks towards the bottom in per capita health spending, as well as in state Medicaid support, employer-based coverage, and percentage of uninsured.

Healthcare costs have been on the rise in California and across the USA, outpacing inflation, GDP, and household income. From 1980 to 2010, healthcare spending per capita in the USA expanded roughly eight times in terms of purchasing power, compared to a five-fold increase for most Western European countries. Two-thirds of this hefty rise can be attributed to a greater use of advanced medical technology, including expensive new drugs. Other key factors are worsening rates of obesity and chronic health conditions, and the higher cost of administering a system driven by private insurance versus a national healthcare model.

The burden of rising healthcare costs is borne by all sectors—families, employers, and governments. Unfortunately, overall healthcare spending per capita in California has lagged behind the growth of healthcare spending per capita in the USA as a whole. Worse, California ranks last, roughly 33 percent below the US average, in per capita spending on Medi-Cal, the state-supported Medicaid program for low-income, disabled, and certain elderly people.

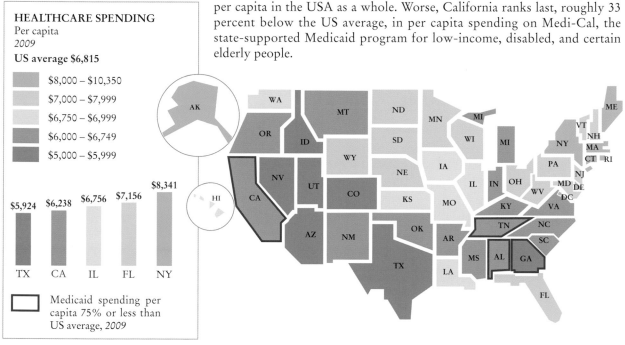

HEALTHCARE SPENDING
Per capita
2009

US average $6,815

- $8,000 – $10,350
- $7,000 – $7,999
- $6,750 – $6,999
- $6,000 – $6,749
- $5,000 – $5,999

TX	CA	IL	FL	NY
$5,924	$6,238	$6,756	$7,156	$8,341

Medicaid spending per capita 75% or less than US average, *2009*

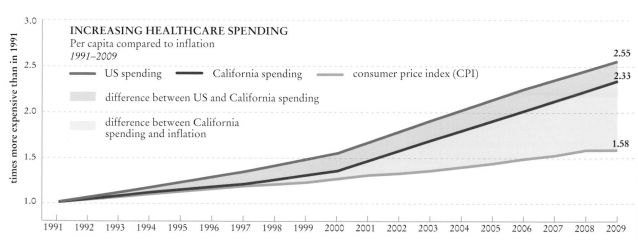

INCREASING HEALTHCARE SPENDING
Per capita compared to inflation
1991–2009

— US spending   — California spending   — consumer price index (CPI)

difference between US and California spending

difference between California spending and inflation

times more expensive than in 1991

2.55
2.33
1.58

Access to healthcare has been declining in California. Employer-sponsored health insurance coverage for working people has dropped from 62 percent to 53 percent over the last decade, putting the state near the bottom in that category. During the same period, the percentage of children and adults enrolled in Medi-Cal has grown from 13 percent to 20 percent as these people have sought alternatives to private insurance.

Meanwhile, the number of uninsured Californians has risen from 19 to 22 percent, leaving roughly 7.3 million people without coverage—some of the highest figures in the country. The uninsured are relatively young (60% are under age 40) and healthy, but the potential for financial disaster or neglect of chronic ills is great. Already, a high volume of emergency room visits is driven by uninsured and poorly insured patients lacking regular care. Contrary to popular perceptions, non-citizens and unauthorized immigrants do not disproportionately utilize safety-net healthcare institutions.

With the passage of the Federal Affordable Care Act, or ObamaCare, in 2010, California is preparing for near-universal insurance coverage of all citizens, regardless of age or pre-existing conditions. This will be achieved through expansion of the Medi-Cal program and creation of a healthcare marketplace (for moderate-income people to purchase subsidized insurance). The federal government will bear the full cost of expansion for the first three years and 90 percent of the cost thereafter.

HEALTH INSURANCE STATUS
As percentage of non-elderly population in selected states *2011*
- uninsured
- receiving employer-based coverage
- other

Texas 26% 52%   Florida 24% 53%

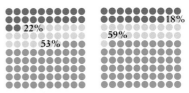

California 22% 53%   US average 18% 59%

New Jersey 18% 67%   New York 14% 59%

Massachusetts 4% 71%

HEALTH INSURANCE COVERAGE IN CALIFORNIA
For non-elderly population
2000 & 2011

2000   2011

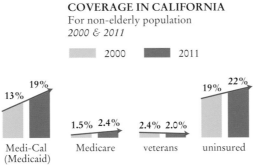

62%   53%   7.3% 7.6%   13% 19%   1.5% 2.4%   2.4% 2.0%   19% 22%

employment-based   individually purchased   Medi-Cal (Medicaid)   Medicare   veterans   uninsured

— private —   — public —

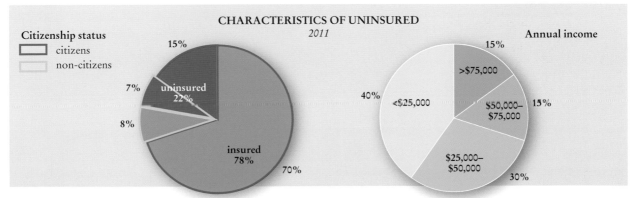

CHARACTERISTICS OF UNINSURED
2011

Citizenship status
- citizens
- non-citizens

15%   7%   uninsured 22%   8%   insured 78%   70%

Annual income

15%   >$75,000 $50,000–$75,000   15%   40%   <$25,000 $25,000–$50,000   30%

PRE-K EDUCATION

Despite its leadership in introducing a variety of early childhood education and support programs, California provides preschool access to only half of its three and four year olds, and quality access to even fewer.

When California introduced the State Preschool Program in 1965 it was one of the first US states to do so. That same year the federal government launched Head Start to provide comprehensive education, health, and social services to disadvantaged children and their families. In 2007, California established the Prekindergarten and Family Literacy Program for the most needy children, followed in 2010 by two-year Transitional Kindergartens to prepare children better for kindergarten and first grade.

Today, there are 11 public-funded early childhood education (ECE) programs in California, providing subsidized childcare and education to working families, parenting teens, and agricultural workers. ECE research has established that high-quality early education yields long-term benefits to children and to society—boosting graduation and employment rates while reducing teen pregnancy and violent crime. Estimates are that every dollar invested in a young child reaps more than seven dollars in return.

Nevertheless, state-subsidized childcare programs serve only 34 percent of income-eligible three year olds and 65 percent of income-eligible four year olds. Counting all public and private ECE centers, only 47 percent (close to the US average) of three and four year olds attend preschool in California, and participation is much lower in low- and middle-income regions. Fortunately, linguistically isolated four year olds, where both parents do not speak English well, are able to participate in center-based care at roughly the same rate as other children. On the other hand, California State Preschools are able to meet only three of the ten quality benchmarks that include learning standards, teacher quality, staff ratio, and health and nutrition support.

California allocates more than the US average per child to preschool programs, but the cost is much higher than in most states. Childcare Aware America has established that California is one of the least affordable states for infant care, but that the situation improves for three and four year olds. In 2011 to 2012, the California Report Card by Childrennow.org assigned a grade of C minus to the area of early learning and development. The state needs to do more to meet the ambitious vision of providing quality preschool programs, as recognized by President Obama in his 2012 State of the Union address.

CALIFORNIA PRE-K PROVISION
For low-income families
2008

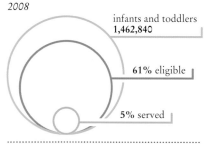

infants and toddlers
1,462,840

61% eligible

5% served

3 year olds
542,338

53% eligible

18% served

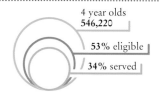

4 year olds
546,220

53% eligible

34% served

PRE-K EDUCATION: AFFORDABILITY, ACCESS, AND QUALITY
In selected US states
2009–11

 average annual cost of full-time care by state of 4 year old at childcare center, *2011*

 state money allocated per child enrolled, *2011*

 percentage of 3 and 4 year olds enrolled in preschool, *2009–11*

 number of quality benchmarks met (out of 10), *2010–11*

US average includes access and quality information from 11 states that do not provide any state pre-K school program.

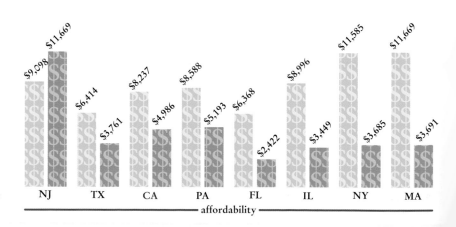

NJ	TX	CA	PA	FL	IL	NY	MA
$9,098 $11,669	$6,414 $3,761	$8,237 $4,986	$8,588 $5,193	$6,368 $2,422	$8,996 $3,449	$11,585 $3,685	$11,669 $3,691

— affordability —

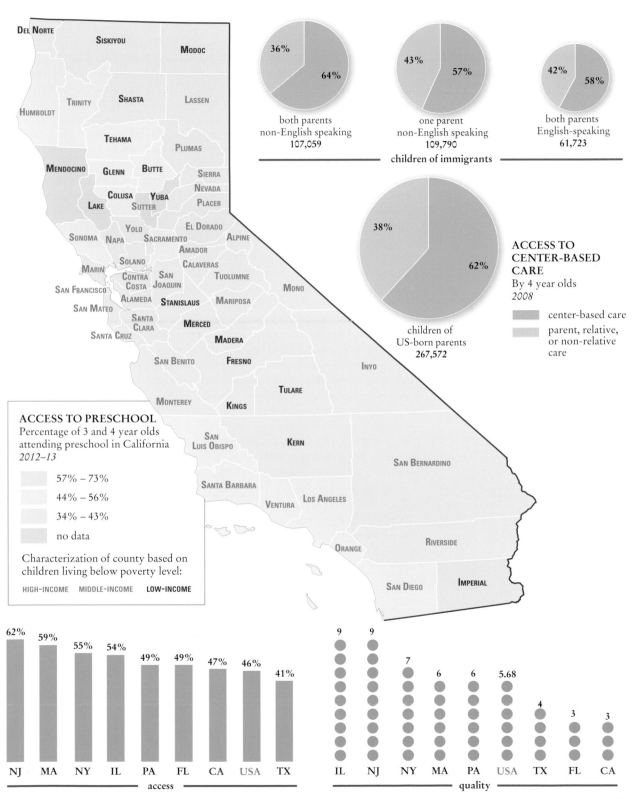

K–12 EDUCATION

California's once-heralded K–12 public education system today ranks near the bottom in student achievement, graduation rates, student–teacher ratio, and per-pupil funding. Greatly increased investment and commitment are needed to put public schooling back on a sound footing.

California educates more than 6 million K–12 students in 8,000 public schools distributed over close to 1,000 school districts. About 5 percent of these students attend 800 publicly funded charter schools, subject to fewer state regulations. In addition, roughly 10 percent of California students attend private schools, home schools, or religious schools. Unfortunately, the public education system is falling short of its historical goal of preparing the young for democratic citizenry and economic success.

In 2011 The Nation's Report Card ranked California's fourth and eighth graders at 46th place in math and reading and 48th place in science. The National Center for Educational Statistics ranked California at the bottom in student–teacher ratio at the secondary-school level. The performance of California's public education system is consistent with the poor rating of US students overall in the OECD PISA study of 70 countries—mediocre in reading and science and below average in mathematics. Since World War II, when the US was ranked number 1 in high-school graduation rate, it has slipped to 22nd among 27 industrialized countries.

Although the California Department of Education reports that there has been a steady improvement in proficiency by all racial groups over the last decade, by roughly 20 percentage points, a survey of more than 250 high-school principals points to significant challenges facing California's public education system: less attention to students from teachers and counselors, fewer instructional materials, less diverse and engaging curriculum, declining progress to graduation and pathways to college, and increasing inequality across and within schools.

Funding of public education has fallen badly over the last 30 years. Whereas California used to be among the top states in spending per pupil for K–12 schools, the Quality Counts 2013 Report ranked California in 48th place in per-student expenditure (adjusted for regional cost differences). California's school finance system is also highly inequitable, with wide

PATHWAY TO COLLEGE
Percentage of 9th-grade students in California who completed each subsequent stage
Class of 2009

all students
Latino students
African-American students

9th Grade
100%
100%
100%

10th Grade
91%
87%
83%

11th Grade
83%
77%
73%

12th Grade
77%
68%
66%

high-school graduates (2009)
67%
57%
52%

eligible for CSU and UC
26%
16%
16%

Community College 1st Year
20%
15%
12%

CSU 1st Year
8%
6%
6%

UC 1st Year
5%
2%
2%

VARIATION IN FUNDING PER PUPIL
Between School Districts with 1,000 or more pupils
2011
Counties with 10 or more such districts   extent of variation

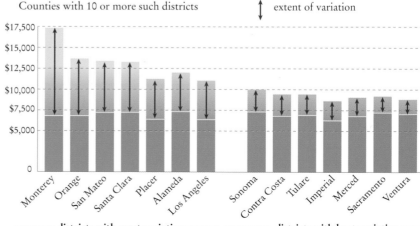

— districts with most variation —   — districts with least variation —

variation in per student funding among school districts, ranging from a low of $6,100 to a high of $17,450, for districts with more than 1,000 students. The finance system is considered unfair, complex, and bureaucratic.

California needs to restore former high levels of public-school funding and revamp its public education system in light of international best practices—setting rigorous standards for students, using empirical material to improve instruction, concentrating resources on the most challenged students, and investing heavily in teacher training. Above all, schools should be recruiting teachers with the passion and skills for the profession and for working with young people.

EXPENDITURE PER PUPIL
Adjusted for regional cost differences
2010

- $15,000 or more
- $13,500 – $14,999
- $11,825 – $13,499

US average: $11,824

- $10,500 – $11,824
- $9,000 – $10,499
- less than $9,000

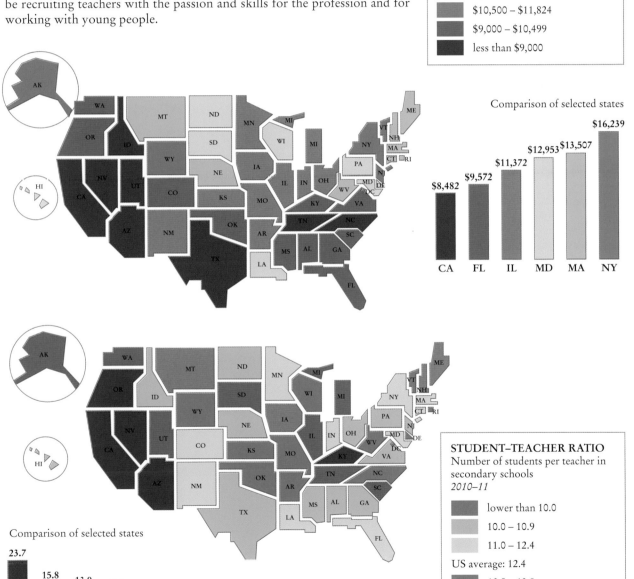

Comparison of selected states

	CA	FL	IL	MD	MA	NY
	$8,482	$9,572	$11,372	$12,953	$13,507	$16,239

Comparison of selected states

	CA	UT	IA	NY	NJ	WV
	23.7	15.8	13.9	12.3	10.6	7.5

STUDENT–TEACHER RATIO
Number of students per teacher in secondary schools
2010–11

- lower than 10.0
- 10.0 – 10.9
- 11.0 – 12.4

US average: 12.4

- 12.5 – 13.9
- 14.0 – 15.9
- 16.0 or higher

97

Higher Education

California's public universities, vital engines of economic and civic life, are in danger of failing to provide affordable access to quality higher education. Can California rediscover its former commitment to public higher education?

GOVERNMENT FUNDING FOR HIGHER EDUCATION
Share by type of institution
2000 & 2010

- ■ University of California
- ■ California State University
- ▨ California Community Colleges

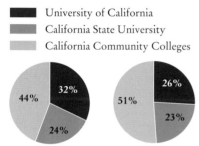

2000 — 44%, 32%, 24%
2010 — 26%, 23%, 51%

CHANGING PRIORITIES
Share of state general fund
1967 & 2011

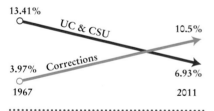

13.41% UC & CSU 10.5%
3.97% Corrections 6.93%
1967 — 2011

California's system of higher education was long the envy of the world. Not only are its top private universities—Stanford and CalTech—among the best, its public colleges and universities were once unrivaled. Berkeley is considered the country's finest public university and the other nine campuses of the University of California (UC) are not far behind. UC educates over 200,000 students a year, as well as carrying out path-breaking research across hundreds of fields. The 23 campuses of the California State University (CSU) enroll over 300,000 students. The Community College system is the country's largest, with 2.6 million students at 112 campuses. Millions of Californians are graduates of public higher education, contributing to the state's economic and civic dynamism.

California was an early adopter of the state college (1868) and junior college ideas (1906), but the greatest buildup came after World War II, with dozens of new campuses. The era was marked by the Master Plan for Higher Education (1960), with its three pillars of access, affordability, and quality. Until recently, college tuition was nominal. This world-class system is now under threat, with budget cuts of up to one-third during the recession.

Tuition fees skyrocketed as state funding collapsed under the pressure of fiscal deficits. Although public education has suffered across the US, tuition and living cost increases have been much sharper in California. UC is now one of the most expensive public universities in the country and students contribute a roughly equal share of total funding to that of the state. The result is heavy financial pressure on students, the majority of whom are young people of color. Student and family debt loads are rising.

With cutbacks in classes, hundreds of thousands of students have been turned away from public colleges and universities and find their progress to degree level delayed. UC campuses are admitting more out-of-state students in search of higher revenue. Progression from high school to CSU and UC declined from 22 to 18 percent from 2006 to 2010, even though the readiness of graduates held steady. The reduction of highly prepared K–12 finishers going to UC and CSU was sharper, from 67 to 55 percent. The Master Plan's promise of entry into the UC system for the top 12.5 percent of high school graduates is at stake.

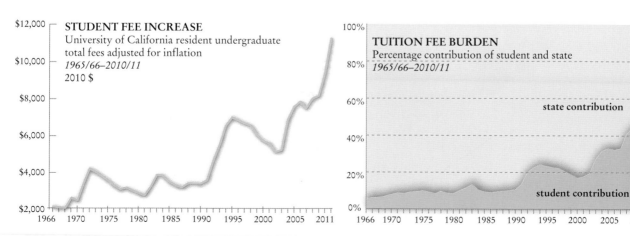

STUDENT FEE INCREASE
University of California resident undergraduate total fees adjusted for inflation
1965/66–2010/11
2010 $

TUITION FEE BURDEN
Percentage contribution of student and state
1965/66–2010/11

state contribution

student contribution

Yet, California's workforce needs an estimated 1 million more college graduates to compensate for retiring baby-boomers in the coming years. President Obama has set an ambitious goal of 60 percent of American adults aged 25 to 34 years old earning a college degree by 2020. Because of mass immigration and school dropouts, California has fallen into the bottom half of US states in terms of its percentage of college graduates, and it will need an additional 1 million degree-earners to meet the US goal. Can California rediscover its past commitment to higher education, so vital to its leadership in economic and civic life?

COLLEGE DEGREE COMPARISON
Percentage of 25–34 year olds with college degree
2010

	49.3% or more
	44.3% – 49.2%
	39.3% – 44.2%

US average: 39.3%

	34.3% – 39.2%
	29.3% – 34.2%
	28.3% – 29.2%

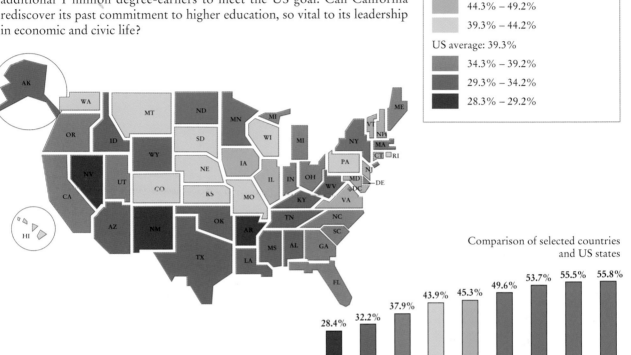

Comparison of selected countries and US states

NV	TX	CA	PA	IL	NY	Japan	South Korea	Canada
28.4%	32.2%	37.9%	43.9%	45.3%	49.6%	53.7%	55.5%	55.8%

ECONOMIC VALUE OF HIGHER EDUCATION
For population 25 years or older
2009

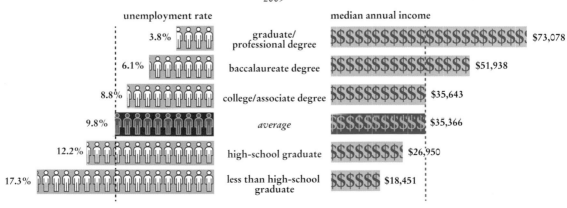

unemployment rate		median annual income
3.8%	graduate/professional degree	$73,078
6.1%	baccalaureate degree	$51,938
8.8%	college/associate degree	$35,643
9.8%	*average*	$35,366
12.2%	high-school graduate	$26,950
17.3%	less than high-school graduate	$18,451

Chapter Eight

INEQUALITY &
SOCIAL DIVIDES

Today the United States is by far the most unequal rich democracy and California is at its leading edge. The distribution of income and wealth in the US was remarkably stable from 1945 to 1975. Since then, the gap between rich and poor has widened steadily, prompting serious debate about the impacts of economic inequality, and providing growing evidence of its profound costs.

A popular view in California and elsewhere is that the unequal accumulation of investment resources promotes innovation and creative risk-taking, and that the state's ability to attract and reward the brightest talent (from India, China, and elsewhere) and the cheapest labor (particularly from Latin America) contributes to its technological and agricultural growth. It is not clear, however, that these rationales for rewarding innovation can be extended to the extraordinary levels of inequality now reached.

Inequality marks many key social divides in California. The young and the old are more likely to feel the sting of poverty, while gays, the disabled, and the homeless suffer particular indignities of enmity, neglect, and exclusion. The broadest strokes of persistent inequality are drawn along the lines of race and gender.

David Moss has found that "more equal societies had longer periods of sustained economic growth than unequal ones." In comparative studies across developed countries and the United States, Richard Wilkinson has shown that higher inequality reduces social mobility and exacerbates a wide range of health and social problems, including mental illness, homicide, obesity, mortality, bullying, and incarceration. Poverty damages individuals and society by preventing those at the bottom from realizing their potential, by depriving them of their freedoms and capabilities, as Amartya Sen has argued. Great economic inequalities also intensify the bias of political institutions toward the rich, undermining democracy.

The sociologist Goran Therborn defines inequalities as differences we consider unjust. Social conditions are raised to the level of injustice when they violate a moral norm and when the inequality is capable of being changed. When five percent of adults possess more than half of the wealth, one in six children go hungry, close to 100,000 people sleep every night on the streets, one in four families lack health insurance, and a Latino woman gets less than half the pay of a White man, we need to ask ourselves: what kind of civilized society do we want to build?

Homeless people
sort through recycling
bins in downtown
San Diego.

INCOME, WEALTH, & POVERTY

Income and wealth inequality have grown significantly in the last 30 years, fueled by stagnant wages, rising assets values and corporate pay, as well as federal tax relief for the rich. Poverty is rampant in California despite its wealth and prosperity.

Inequality has risen rapidly in California and in the United States since the mid-1970s and may now be greater than even in the Gilded Age or Roaring Twenties. Inequality in the USA is the highest of all rich countries, and among the worst in the world. California is at the leading edge of this unhappy development.

The main reason for rising inequality has been enrichment at the top. Executive pay has multiplied several times over, while the top 20 percent of skilled labor in management and technology have seen their salaries climb. The growth of wealth has also come from the rising value of stocks and other financial assets; the top 10 percent own 73 percent of all assets. California's super-rich have done very well indeed, and the state is home to more millionaires and billionaires than any other state.

Meanwhile, wages and salaries of middle-level households have been flat, and those at the bottom have fallen in real terms, as has the wealth of large numbers of families. Houses and cars are the principal assets of the lower 80 percent, and homeownership has fallen in California over the last generation, while millions of families saw the value of their homes collapse in the Great Recession.

HOW CALIFORNIA COMPARES

Gini coefficient of inequality
latest year available 2005–11
selected countries

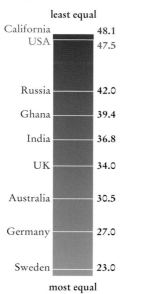

least equal

California	48.1
USA	47.5
Russia	42.0
Ghana	39.4
India	36.8
UK	34.0
Australia	30.5
Germany	27.0
Sweden	23.0

most equal

RISING CEO-TO-WORKER COMPENSATION RATIO

Number of times by which CEO compensation is greater than average US worker's compensation
1965–2011

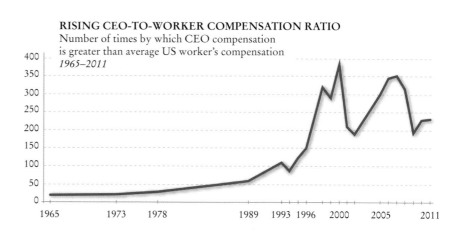

WIDENING GAP BETWEEN RICH AND POOR IN USA

- median household
- top 1%

1:19 ratio of poor to rich

Change in income inequality
2009 $

1987	2009
$778,000	$1,200,000
1:19	1:34
$41,030	$35,740

Change in wealth inequality
2010 $

1983	2010
$9,599,000	$16,439,000
1:131	1:288
$73,000	$57,000

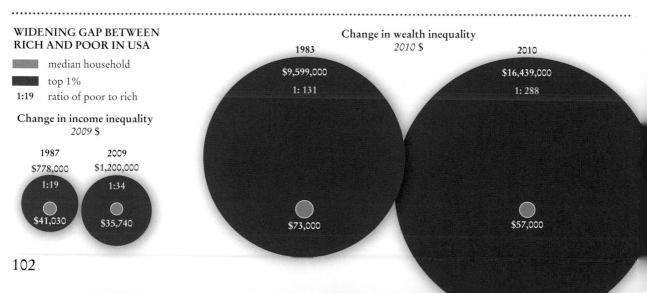

The generous income, capital gains, and estate taxation relief awarded during the Reagan–Bush era helped the rich in the US amass unsurpassed wealth. The top marginal federal income tax rate fell from 91 percent during the 1950s to 28 percent in the 2000s, and California followed suit. Proposition 13 cut taxes on commercial property, also favoring wealth accumulation.

While some inequality may benefit the economy by rewarding risk and innovation, excessive inequality is detrimental to growth by depressing demand; moreover, it is politically corrosive, fueling the power of money in elections and legislation, and socially divisive, creating a chasm between classes. California's economy and government both performed better in the postwar era when equality was greater and taxation more progressive.

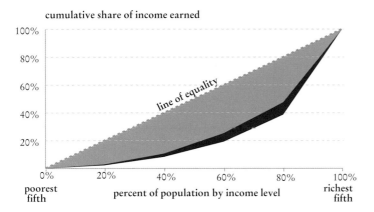

cumulative share of income earned

line of equality

poorest fifth

richest fifth

percent of population by income level

INCREASING INCOME INEQUALITY IN CALIFORNIA
1987–2009

income inequality in 1987

increased income inequality 1987–2009

Greater inequality has pushed millions of Californians into poverty. By the traditional federal poverty rate, California ranks among the ten worst states, and a new poverty measure, which takes into account the cost of living and government assistance programs, ranks California dead last in 2012. The state's 24 percent poverty rate far exceeds the US average. California offers CalWorks, a cash assistance and welfare program for the needy, but eligibility criteria, work rules, and budget cuts have left out a significant majority of the impoverished.

POVERTY RATE
By state
2009–11

23.5%

17.0% – 19.9%

14.0% – 16.9%
US average: 15.8%

11.0% – 13.9%

8.4% – 10.9%

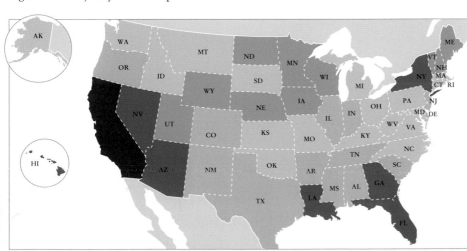

HUNGER & HOMELESSNESS

Millions of Californians go hungry every day and tens of thousands are homeless. This is one of the worst records in the nation. Government food assistance programs that help mitigate hunger need to be strengthened. Homeless people have little institutional support and often face hostility.

California ranks in the bottom ten states for hunger, or food insecurity. Roughly 4 million adults and 2.5 million children—or one-sixth of the population—worry about where their next meal will come from and their inability to afford a balanced diet. The UCLA Health Policy Institute reports that there has been roughly a 50 percent increase in food-insecure adult Californians over the last decade and that 1.4 million suffer from *very low* food security, where meals are regularly missed for lack of money.

Hunger leads to poor physiological and mental health and to poor learning in children. Ironically, hunger can also provoke obesity due to high-fat, sugary foods being relatively inexpensive. Food insecurity is primarily caused by extreme poverty and unemployment, not by ignorance about healthy food, as is often thought.

Food assistance is provided by the state CalFresh program (formerly known as Food Stamps) and the federal WIC program (Women, Infants, and Children), in addition to several lunch programs. These efforts subsidize households on low incomes, but fewer than half of eligible families participate. Elimination of excessive requirements such as fingerprinting could improve participation and reduce costs.

California hosts the largest homeless population in the nation—about 130,000 people. More than 25 percent are chronically homeless (compared with the national average of 16 percent), and 65 percent are unsheltered. Unemployment and unaffordable housing are the leading causes of homelessness, followed by substance abuse, unstable family life, and mental and physical illness. Remarkably, over 40 percent of homeless have some kind of job, and many are in families and live out of their cars. The cost of homelessness to the public is quite high, because of frequent hospitalization, medical treatment, police intervention, and emergency shelter provision.

While the public generally favors aid to the ill-fed, there is much less support for the homeless. A federal government program to combat homelessness was begun in 1988 and terminated a few years later. Most of the expense of caring for the homeless falls on cities, counties, and non-profit organizations. While some communities are more tolerant of the homeless, even the most progressive cities, like Berkeley and Santa Cruz, have stringent laws against loitering, begging, and sleeping in public.

US HOMELESS
Share by state
2012

Total: 633,782

California total: 131,193 — 21%

chronic homeless 25%

New York 11%

Florida 9%

Texas 5.4%

others 29%

Washington 3.2%

Georgia 3.2%

HOMELESS IN CALIFORNIA
Selected areas
2011

LA City & County

42,353

San Diego City & County

10,013

San Jose, Santa Clara City & County

7,053

Santa Ana, Anaheim, Orange County

7,010

Riverside City & County

6,096

CHARACTERISTICS OF LOS ANGELES' HOMELESS
2009

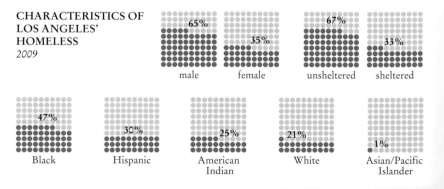

male 65%   female 35%

unsheltered 67%   sheltered 33%

Black 47%

Hispanic 30%

American Indian 25%

White 21%

Asian/Pacific Islander 1%

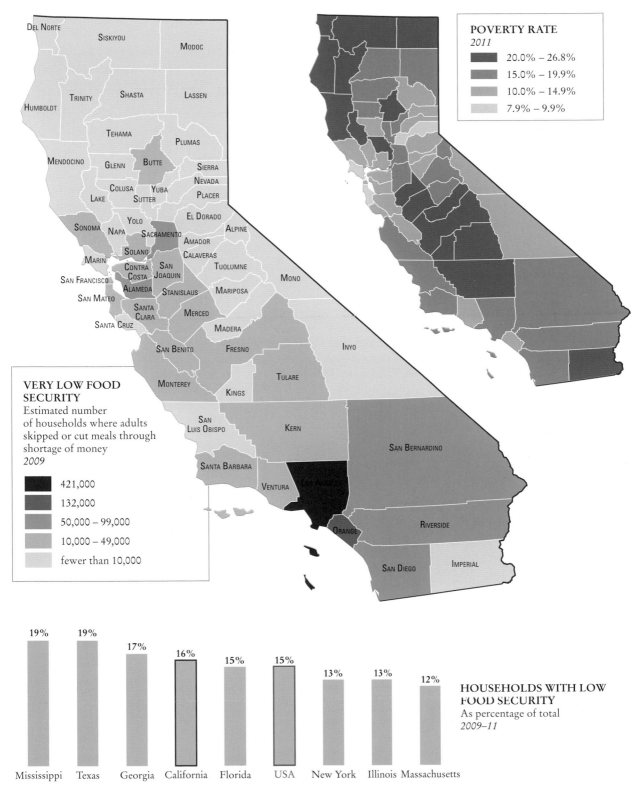

POVERTY RATE
2011

- 20.0% – 26.8%
- 15.0% – 19.9%
- 10.0% – 14.9%
- 7.9% – 9.9%

VERY LOW FOOD SECURITY
Estimated number of households where adults skipped or cut meals through shortage of money
2009

- 421,000
- 132,000
- 50,000 – 99,000
- 10,000 – 49,000
- fewer than 10,000

Del Norte	Siskiyou	Modoc

HOUSEHOLDS WITH LOW FOOD SECURITY
As percentage of total
2009–11

Mississippi 19%
Texas 19%
Georgia 17%
California 16%
Florida 15%
USA 15%
New York 13%
Illinois 13%
Massachusetts 12%

RACE & ETHNICITY

California enjoys a rich mix of people of different races and national origins, just one of four states where minorities are the majority. Yet the participation of people of color in politics and business is much less than that of Whites, and almost all suffer disproportionately from low incomes, poor health, and less education.

I n California, Whites are the minority and people of color the majority—roughly three-fifths of the population (versus one-third nationally). Hispanics/Latinos (37.6%) form the largest group, followed by Asian Americans (12.8%), African Americans (5.8%), and Native Americans and Hawaiian/Pacific Islanders (less than 1%). Only three other states—Texas, New Mexico, Hawaii—have non-White majorities.

People of color are at a disadvantage compared to Whites. They own much less property, including businesses and homes, and are far under-represented among managers and professionals. They form the bulk of California's working people. Even there, they suffer wage gaps ranging from 83 cents for Asian men to 43 cents for Hispanic women (for every dollar paid to White males for comparable work). Latinos, African Americans, and Native Americans are especially afflicted by poverty and unemployment, which lead to poorer access to and outcomes in healthcare, education, and criminal justice, as measured by such indices as obesity, college enrollment, and incarceration. Asians as a whole do better, but many, such as Cambodians and Filipinos, do not.

Politically, California's minorities have long been under-represented. The racial makeup of the state legislature and congressional delegation mirrors percentages among voters, but two-thirds of the electorate are White. Lower voting rates among people of color, particularly Hispanics, are a legacy of immigration (non-citizenship), more youth, low registration, and lack of mobilization. This is changing, putting more Latinos and Asians in prominent positions, as mayors of Los Angeles and San Francisco, or legislative leaders.

Definitions of race and ethnicity are profoundly social, influenced by geographic origin, culture, class, and religion. Most Asian Americans identify with countries not a continent. Hispanics come from many Latin countries, have varying skin color, and speak English or Spanish. Most African Americans have slave origins, but many are recent immigrants. California also has a large number of mixed-race families.

Geographically, there are higher percentages of Whites in Northern California and the Sierra Nevada, Latinos in the Central Valley, and Asians along the coasts.

POVERTY RATE
Among racial groups in California
2012

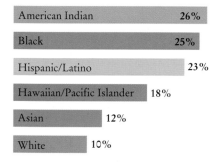

American Indian	26%
Black	25%
Hispanic/Latino	23%
Hawaiian/Pacific Islander	18%
Asian	12%
White	10%

BUSINESS EMPOWERMENT
Racial composition of directors in 85 of California's largest Fortune 1000 Companies
2012

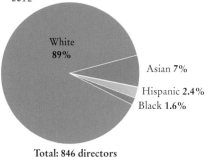

White 89%
Asian 7%
Hispanic 2.4%
Black 1.6%

Total: 846 directors

POLITICAL EMPOWERMENT
Racial composition of California State Legislature
2010

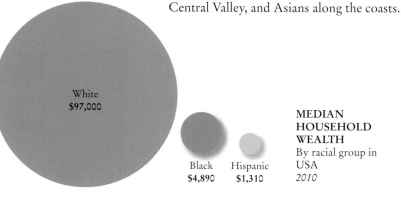

White $97,000
Black $4,890
Hispanic $1,310

MEDIAN HOUSEHOLD WEALTH
By racial group in USA
2010

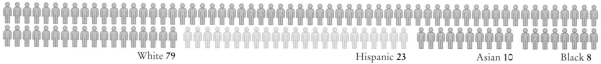

White 79   Hispanic 23   Asian 10   Black 8

Total: 120 legislators in assembly and senate

At finer scales, the races are often sharply segregated, as with African Americans in East Oakland or Salvadorans west of downtown LA. But the old concentration of minorities in inner cities is passing; young Whites have moved back into cities, while immigrants and their children have spilled into suburbs, as in the case of Chinese in Monterey Park and Vietnamese in Garden Grove. Racial segregation is partly due to income differences and social networks, but White preference for exclusive neighborhoods is the principal cause.

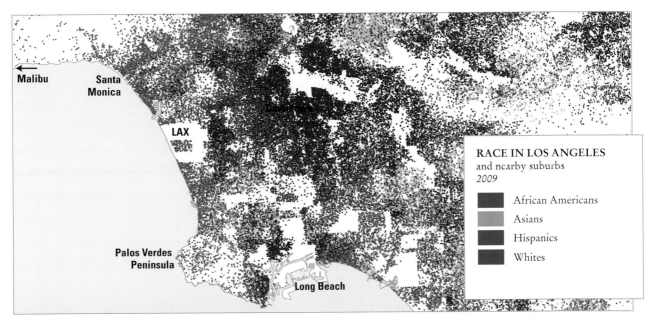

RACE IN LOS ANGELES
and nearby suburbs
2009

African Americans
Asians
Hispanics
Whites

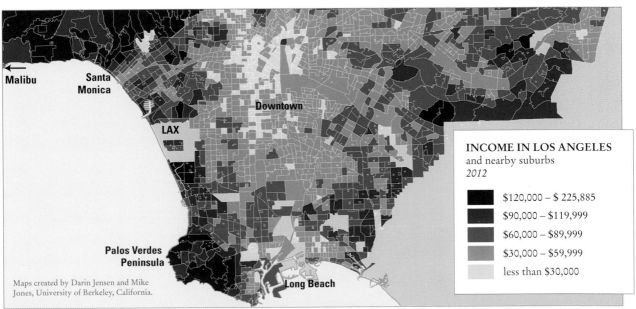

INCOME IN LOS ANGELES
and nearby suburbs
2012

$120,000 – $ 225,885
$90,000 – $119,999
$60,000 – $89,999
$30,000 – $59,999
less than $30,000

Maps created by Darin Jensen and Mike Jones, University of Berkeley, California.

GENDER & SEXUAL ORIENTATION

California's record of gender equity is good in education, moderate in wages and political representation, and poor in business. The state has been a pioneer in the struggle for gay rights, but has suffered setbacks on the question of equal rights to marriage.

California mirrors the nation in its gender gap, with high marks for equality in education and health, lagging in economic opportunity, and poor in political empowerment. The Global Gender Gap Report by the World Economic Forum ranked the US 22nd among 134 countries on these four dimensions of gender equality.

Women are now more likely than men to hold college or graduate degrees. California is the first state to be represented by two women in the US Senate, and it has a higher percentage of women legislators (26.6%) than the US average. But just one-quarter of county supervisors are women and fewer than one in ten city mayors. Little progress has been seen since 2000.

California is in the top five states for the lowest wage gap between men and women, roughly 85 cents on the dollar for the same work. The gender gap is most severe in business and professional leadership. Women represent only 10 percent of directors and top executives in the 400 largest corporations based in the state, of which almost one-third have no women at all in top positions. Santa Clara County (Silicon Valley) and Orange County have the worst records for women executives and directors.

Domestic violence remains a serious problem for women. California has consistently been one of the ten best states in having the lowest rates of violence against women, and yet the California Women's Health Survey found some 40 percent of women experience partner violence in their lifetimes. The Violence Against Women Act (VAWA) passed by Congress in 1994 and expanded in 2013, plus stronger action by local police and courts, has helped reduce domestic violence.

CORPORATE BOARD MEMBERS
Based on 85 of the 400 largest California companies that also appeared in the Fortune 1000 List
2012

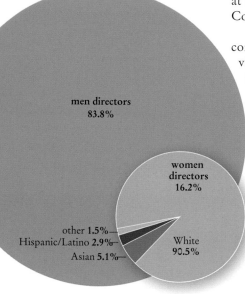

men directors
83.8%

women directors
16.2%

other 1.5%
Hispanic/Latino 2.9%
Asian 5.1%
White 90.5%

GENDER GAP IN USA
Women's experience compared with that of men as measured by Global Gender Gap Index
2012

political empowerment **.156**

economic opportunity **.814**

health **.979**

educational attainment **1.0**

WOMEN IN CALIFORNIA STATE LEGISLATURE
1972–2012

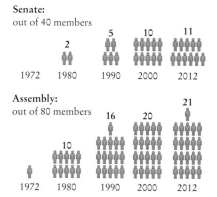

Senate:
out of 40 members

1972	2 / 1980	5 / 1990	10 / 2000	11 / 2012

Assembly:
out of 80 members

| 1972 | 10 / 1980 | 16 / 1990 | 20 / 2000 | 21 / 2012 |

MEDIAN WAGES
By sex and race in California
2011

men   women

wage as % of that of White male

$67,959	$56,611	$51,393	$50,368	$47,795	$47,757	$42,939	$41,759	$41,288	$36,089	$32,042	$29,347
	83%	76%	74%	70%	70%	63%	61%	61%	53%	47%	43%
White	Asian	White	all	Black	Asian	Black	all	American Indian	American Indian	Hispanic	Hispanic

The Lesbian, Gay, Bisexual, and Transgender (LGBT) population of California is the largest in the country. San Francisco has the highest percentage of LGBT people among major US metro areas and was for many years known as the "Gay Capital of the US", while Los Angeles, with an estimated 282,500 LGBT people, has the second-highest such population after New York. The gay population is younger and more educated than the average.

The LGBT community has long suffered discrimination and prosecution. Not until 1974 was the California Constitution amended to recognize gay rights. The first American gay and lesbian rights organizations were founded in Los Angeles and San Francisco in the 1950s. When Harvey Milk was elected Supervisor in San Francisco in 1977, he was the first openly gay public officer in California; but he was assassinated the next year. Hate crimes against gays are surprisingly prevalent, second only to those based on race.

The right of same-sex couples to marry has been a burning issue in recent years, and same-sex marriage has been approved in eight states. In 1999, California adopted a domestic partnership law, but Proposition 22 in 2000 declared marriage exclusively heterosexual. That law was struck down by the California Supreme Court in 2008, triggering another anti-gay marriage act, Proposition 8. That, too, has been ruled unconstitutional by lower courts and is now before the US Supreme Court.

Notwithstanding these setbacks, attitudes are rapidly changing, especially among the young. Gay marriage is now favored by the majority in opinion polls and is increasingly normalized in everyday life, as exemplified by the more than 50,000 children being raised by gay couples around the state.

HATE CRIMES IN CALIFORNIA
Number of incidents by type of bias or motivation
2011

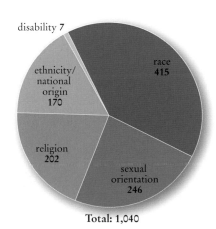

Total: 1,040

VIEWS ON GAY MARRIAGE
By age groups
2008

- For (No to Proposition 8)
- Against (Yes to Proposition 8)

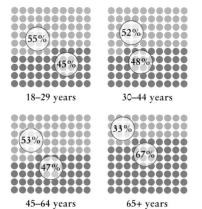

LGBT HISTORY IN CALIFORNIA
1850–2012

- legislative action or action by authorities
- events by gay community
- political events

1850	California becomes part of USA. California law criminalizes sexual orientation.
1914	Vagrancy law is introduced against certain same-sex activities.
1950	First American Sustained Gay Group, The Mattachine Society, is founded in Los Angeles.
1955	First major American Lesbian Group, Daughters of Bilitis, is founded in San Francisco.
1961	Vagrancy law is replaced by a "disorderly conduct" law.
1964	*LIFE* magazine declares San Francisco as "Gay Capital of the US".
1970	First Gay Pride Parade is held in Los Angeles.
1972	San Francisco becomes one of the first cities to pass homosexual rights ordinance.
1974	California Constitution is amended, turning the tide in favor of LGBT rights.
1977	Harvey Milk is elected county-supervisor in San Francisco.
1978	Anti-Gay Briggs Initiative to ban gay school teachers is defeated.
1978	Harvey Milk is assassinated by Dan White.
1979	Dan White is acquitted; White Night Riots in San Francisco.
1982	Laguna Beach elects the first openly gay mayor in US history.
1984	Berkeley adopts domestic partnership health benefits.
1994	Sheila Kuehl becomes the first openly LGBT member of the state legislature.
1999	California adopts a domestic partnership law.
2000	California passes Proposition 22 denying same-sex marriage rights.
2008	California Supreme Court strikes down Proposition 22.
	California voters pass Proposition 8 denying same-sex marriage rights.
2011	California passes a bill to introduce LGBT history in public schools.

YOUTH & OLD AGE

California's young and old suffer disproportionately from deprivation, and many are ineligible for government benefits because of inadequate measures of cost of living and need.

Children and the elderly are the most vulnerable Californians. The state has a relatively youthful population, but its children are not doing well. The poverty rate for children is much higher (over 23%) than the average for all Californians (almost 16%), and in revised poverty measures that include a wider range of costs for food, housing, education, and nutrition, the state's youngest citizens fare even worse (almost 29% in poverty). Children who experience prolonged economic hardship are at the greatest risk of poor educational, health, and economic life chances. Among California's youth, drug use, crime, violence, bullying, and gang membership are common. Almost two-thirds of poor children live with working adults, who are unable to provide a minimum level of support for their families—California is one of 26 states that do not offer earned income-tax credit to help working families—and the state has tens of thousands of children in foster care or homeless.

High costs of housing and healthcare are the primary sources of economic risk for elders, and those living alone are at much greater risk than couples—single elderly women even more so. Figures on elder poverty based on the federal poverty index are misleading. A California Elder Security Standard developed by the Insight Center for Community Economic Development estimates that roughly double the federal poverty line is the income required to meet the basic needs of elders. Based on this index, in 2007 some 47 percent of California elders—about 1.8 million people—needed assistance, compared to the official rate of 8 percent below the federal poverty line. The number of elderly is projected to double in the next 15 years to more than 8.5 million.

AGE DISTRIBUTION
In California
2011

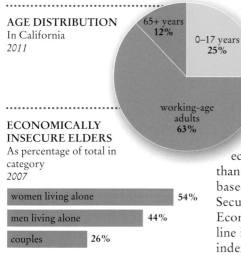

65+ years 12%
0–17 years 25%
working-age adults 63%

ECONOMICALLY INSECURE ELDERS
As percentage of total in category
2007

women living alone	54%
men living alone	44%
couples	26%

CHILDREN IN NEED
Percentage of those aged 0–17 years
latest data available 2009–12

no health insurance
12%

special healthcare needs
15%

food insecure
17%

living in poverty
23%

45% of children living with a **single mother** are living in **poverty**

YOUNG PEOPLE AT RISK
Percentage age 16–17 recently exhibiting specified behavior
2009–11

- 11th grade in public schools
- continuation, community day, or other alternative school types

carried a gun at school	engaged in fighting at school	experienced cyber-bullying	gang involvement	binge drinking	heavy drug user	seriously considered attempting suicide
4% / 14%	15% / 34%	21% / 25%	8% / 15%	22% / 43%	13% / 34%	17% / 21%

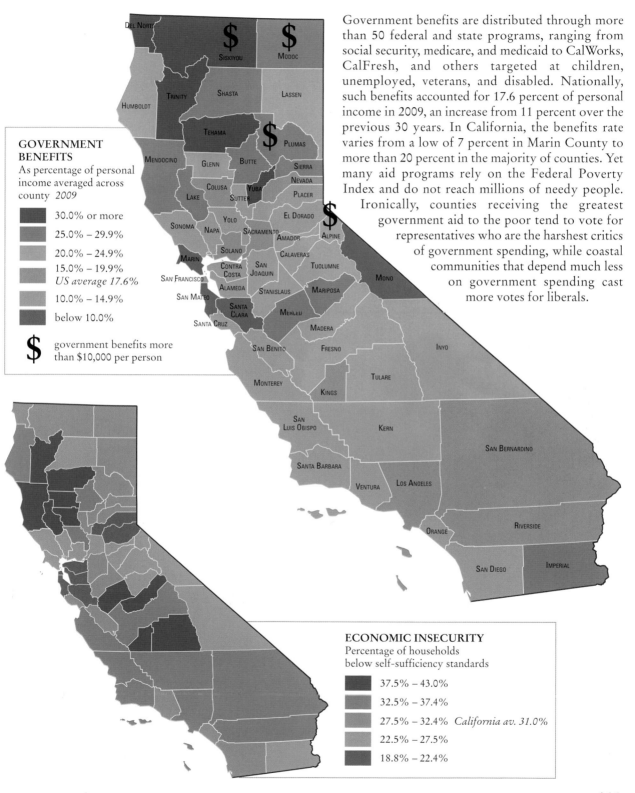

Government benefits are distributed through more than 50 federal and state programs, ranging from social security, medicare, and medicaid to CalWorks, CalFresh, and others targeted at children, unemployed, veterans, and disabled. Nationally, such benefits accounted for 17.6 percent of personal income in 2009, an increase from 11 percent over the previous 30 years. In California, the benefits rate varies from a low of 7 percent in Marin County to more than 20 percent in the majority of counties. Yet many aid programs rely on the Federal Poverty Index and do not reach millions of needy people.

Ironically, counties receiving the greatest government aid to the poor tend to vote for representatives who are the harshest critics of government spending, while coastal communities that depend much less on government spending cast more votes for liberals.

GOVERNMENT BENEFITS

As percentage of personal income averaged across county *2009*

- 30.0% or more
- 25.0% – 29.9%
- 20.0% – 24.9%
- 15.0% – 19.9% *US average 17.6%*
- 10.0% – 14.9%
- below 10.0%

$ government benefits more than $10,000 per person

ECONOMIC INSECURITY
Percentage of households below self-sufficiency standards

- 37.5% – 43.0%
- 32.5% – 37.4%
- 27.5% – 32.4% *California av. 31.0%*
- 22.5% – 27.5%
- 18.8% – 22.4%

Chapter Nine

CHALLENGES AHEAD:
A GLIMPSE INTO
THE FUTURE

GDP PER CAPITA
Largest world economies
2012
PPP $

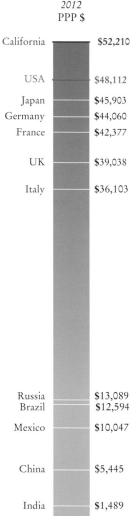

California	$52,210
USA	$48,112
Japan	$45,903
Germany	$44,060
France	$42,377
UK	$39,038
Italy	$36,103
Russia	$13,089
Brazil	$12,594
Mexico	$10,047
China	$5,445
India	$1,489

Elementary-school children
running in park.

California's glory resides in its prosperity, its leadership in technology and innovation, agriculture and industry, and in the promise of opportunity for millions of newcomers. California is a leader in its unmatched efficiency of production as measured by GDP per capita among the largest economies. The lure of California to make it big persists: California stands for growth, for change, for disruption of the status quo. "California is not another American state," concluded Carey McWilliams in his 1949 history *California: The Great Exception*. "It is a revolution within the states." The world watches as California launches bold transportation initiatives, sets ambitious goals to address climate change, invests in new solar power and electric car technologies, integrates millions of new citizens into its economy, and introduces new laws to promote democracy and protect human rights. As the journalist Peter Schrag puts the challenge in *Paradise Lost, California's Experience, America's Future*, "Things had better work in California, where the new American society is first coming into full view, because if it fails here, it may never work anywhere else either."

But there is a dark side. The glorious past of California, with its commitment to free education, open opportunity and widely shared prosperity, is under threat. Income inequality is being pushed to historic extremes. Far too many of the state's children, elderly, disabled, sick, and veterans are poor, hungry, uninsured, and homeless. Will California be able to take care of an elderly population that is about to double in the next 15 years? Must the people of color who now make up the majority of California's population continue to suffer disproportionately?

Immigration to California has stagnated even as new gateways open up elsewhere across the US, but inland migration within California is up sharply to escape high costs of living along the coast. Will the working people of California eventually need to move out of state to realize the American dream of upward mobility or will California embrace them? The world is watching as California's unparalleled diversity unfolds in a time of diminishing opportunity for ordinary people and their children.

California is at a major crossroads. It could seek to emulate leading states such as New York or New Jersey in providing excellent education or Massachusetts in delivering food security and healthcare to residents; or it might simply be content with the above average performance of Illinois and Pennsylvania; or it could very well succumb to the low expectations of Texas and Florida. But California has set much higher expectations for itself on the world's stage.

Some would say that the cure for California lies in its governance, to become free from super-majority requirements that hamper democracy, to remove term-limit restrictions to allow engaged politicians to provide long-term professional leadership, and invest more in education, health, and social infrastructure—not to mention taking such bold steps as the controversial and expensive high-speed rail link between north and south. But can California continue to be governed through a dizzying array of ballot initiatives, too often funded by rich, unaccountable interests? Can the citizenry be persuaded to moderate Proposition 13 and other tax-revolt measures to allow corporate income and property taxes to be raised, as recommended by a business and higher-education consortium? And will business groups be persuaded that California's best future lies in innovation and prosperous consumers rather than the race to the bottom with poorer states and countries?

What would it take to shake up the citizens of California? The Institute for the Future, in an attempt to provoke engagement, surmises that a water infrastructure breakdown or a major earthquake could potentially segregate California into rich and poor enclaves, or an unprecedented collaboration between socially networked communities could take over the government and business functions to work towards the greater good for all. In yet another scenario, California may have to grind down its consumption through austerity while focusing investment on education, health, and basic infrastructure.

In the most futuristic scenario, California is poised to invent the technology to alter the way we interact with each other and with the world in ways that defy imagination. Smart machines with embedded intelligence, contextual awareness, and sensitive feedback mechanisms will invade everyday lives. Change and disruption will be the norm not an exception.

HOW DOES CALIFORNIA COMPARE?
In ranking of selected US states
2009–12
latest year data available

CA   FL
IL   MA
NJ   NY
PA   TX

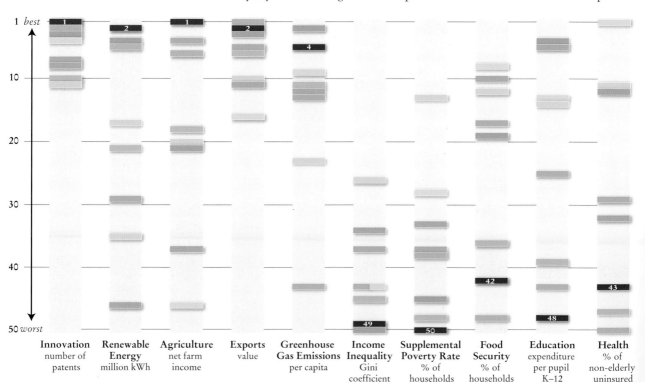

1 *best*

10

20

30

40

50 *worst*

| Innovation | Renewable Energy | Agriculture | Exports | Greenhouse Gas Emissions | Income Inequality | Supplemental Poverty Rate | Food Security | Education | Health |
| number of patents | million kWh | net farm income | value | per capita | Gini coefficient | % of households | % of households | expenditure per pupil K–12 | % of non-elderly uninsured |

114

For example, armed with a deluge of personal health and behavioral data, new health-literate individuals will approach their well-being in such novel ways that healthcare delivery systems will be forced to adapt. Collaboration and navigation of fluid networks will be a vital skill and core competency for the new generation.

California is also being watched on the world stage for its ability to cope with urban gigantism and associated challenges. For the first time in human history, the majority of the world now lives in urban areas. How will California face up to the severe air and water pollution in its cities or limit energy consumption in sprawling metro regions? Will technology be able to reduce traffic congestion through real-time monitoring of clogged highways or reduce movement of workers and goods by reorganizing systems of production? How will California deal with the pernicious effects of inequality in cities, with the rich walled up in favored enclaves while the poor stew in neighborhoods beset by crime, hunger, and homelessness?

In California, the minorities have become the majority in population but not in political engagement, the ranks of voters, or the monied contributors to elections. Will the White minority be willing to yield the reins of government? California has the reputation of being a magnet for creative workers in high-tech industry, but are its own people being prepared to fill the high-end demand for educated, skilled workers? At the same time, given the critical dependence of several key industries on low-skilled immigrants, does California have the will to combat poverty and share future prosperity more inclusively, as it has in the past?

Historian Kevin Starr has declared, optimistically, "Yes, California is saying, Americans of every cultural background can learn to live with and more importantly to respect each other." As California carries out its great experiment in inter-racial, multi-cultural society, economy and democracy, the world waits in suspense.

"There is science, logic, reason; there is thought verified by experience. And then there is California." —Edward Abbey.

POPULATION BY RACE
Percentage of population in each group
1860–2060

White
Hispanic
Asian
Black
American Indian
other

1% 5%
9%
85%
1860
0.4m

0.9%
3% 0.7%
95%
1910
2.4m

0.2%
2% 6%
12%
80%
1960
15.7m

0.4%
2.6%
6%
40%
13%
38%
2010
37.3m

0.4%
4.6%
4%
30%
13%
48%
2060
52.7m

POPULATION BY AGE
Percentage of California
in each age group
1970 & 2030

65+ years   18–64 years   0–17 years

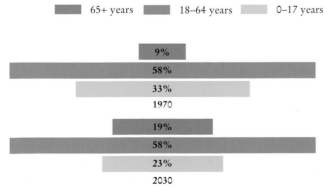

9%
58%
33%
1970

19%
58%
23%
2030

Chapter Ten

DATA CHALLENGES

Despite the availability of data on California from various state and federal agencies, the researcher is confronted by myriad data challenges—inconsistency, reliability, uncertainty, omissions, imperfections, and underlying assumptions. As a result, data must be selected and interpreted with caution.

For example, tracking unauthorized immigrants is a challenge because data cannot be obtained directly. The Department of Homeland Security, Pew Hispanic Center, and Public Policy Institute of California all produce estimates that do not match up. In this case, fortunately, the variation is not large and, given the range of sources, these data gain credence. In contrast, the sharp rise in the number of Native Californians after 1950, as reported by the US Census, remains dubious, even after taking into account domestic migration, shifting definitions, and demographic modeling.

Health data pose a different set of challenges. How to measure good health, for example? We used a numeric score weighing life expectancy and morbidity equally. Quantitative scores of health factors are derived from a combination of clinical care, socioeconomic factors, environment, and behavior. Measurement of health quality is an even a bigger challenge given the unevenness of clinical care. Despite these quandaries, it is vital to have quantitative measures of health quality in view of emerging health markets to provide greater access to healthcare.

In another case, strong resistance to change among water users poses significant challenges in gathering data. Even though the California legislature imposed civic penalties in 2009 for failure to report water diversion and use, large data gaps make it difficult to recommend effective management policies. Water-quality measurement remains in a primitive state, even as our understanding of toxic pollutants and their impacts on health advances too slowly.

Even in the field of energy, where relatively robust data are produced, accounting questions create potential misinterpretation. Small hydro is considered renewable energy under California standards, but most federal reports do not include it. Furthermore, the state includes both in-state and external electricity sources, but many reports include only the former. Depending upon the account, there is a large variation in how much of California's electricity can be attributed to renewables.

Visualization and interpretation of the state of California in every dimension depends upon the validity of underlying data. We are entering a digital age when mind-blowing quantities of data can be collected that may neither be good nor meaningful. This Atlas highlights the importance of good data in several critical areas, including education, resources, demographics, and urbanization, that are essential to California's future well-being.

The mind overwhelmed by data complexity.

DEFINITION OF KEY TERMS

MEASUREMENTS

BTU British Thermal Unit, a measurement of energy.

kWh Kilowatt hour, a unit of energy equal to 1,000 watt hours.

MWh Megawatt hour, a unit of energy equal to 1 million watt hours.

GWh Gigawatt hour. 1GWh = 1,000 MWh; 1 MWh = 1,000 kWh.

MAF Million acre-feet. An acre-foot is the amount of water that would cover a one-acre area to a depth of one foot. One million acre-feet is estimated to be a sufficient annual supply of water for one million families of four. It equates to 325,850 gallons.

PPP Purchasing power parity, used to calculate national incomes so that a dollar has the same purchasing power as a US dollar.

WATER MANAGEMENT

Unimpaired water availability Most precipitated water evaporates. The remainder, known as unimpaired runoff, flows downhill into streams and groundwater basins and becomes available for management and use.

Gross and net water use Gross water use is the water delivered to a home, business, or farm. Some of this water, referred to as recoverable flow, is available for re-use. Net water is gross water less recoverable flow.

Ground water overdraft Perennial yield is the amount of groundwater that can be extracted without lowering groundwater levels over the longterm. Additional annual extraction from a groundwater basin *over a long period of time* above the annual perennial yield is defined as overdraft. Overdraft is not a measure of annual fluctuations in groundwater storage volume. It is a measure of the long-term trend associated with these annual fluctuations.

Hydrologic region California is divided into ten hydrologic regions based on major drainage basins. They are further subdivided into 278 DAUs (detailed analysis units). Data is collected at the DAU level and then aggregated at the hydrologic region by the California Department of Water Resources.

Water demand management Water demand management is a strategy to provide price incentives to consumers to reduce water demand. To make water affordable for basic usage, discounts may be offered for low-income populations to make water access equitable. Furthermore, block pricing is used to keep the prices for the first units low.

Sacramento–San Joaquin River Delta Also known as California Delta. An expansive inland river delta in Northern California near Sacramento and Stockton. The fan-like area of the Delta exits Central Valley through a narrow channel into the San Francisco Bay. The Delta consists of myriad natural and man-made water channels known as sloughs, creating a system of lowland islands and wetlands defined by levees. The Delta is a critical habitat for more than 500 species, hub of major water conveyance system, and its "Thousand Miles of Waterways" is an important recreational resource.

Sacramento Valley 4-River Index This is the sum (in MAF) of Sacramento Rriver inflow at Bend Bridge, Feather River inflow to Lake Oroville, Yuba River at Smartville, and American River inflow to Lake Oroville.

San Joaquin Valley 4-River Index This is the sum (in MAF) of Stanislaus River inflow to New Melones Lake, Tulomne River inflow to New Don Pedro Reservoir, Merced River inflow to Lake McClure, and San Joaquin River inflow to Millerton Lake.

Runoff The movement of rainwater over ground.

Water rights Rights to water in California have historically evolved into a complex regulatory system involving permits and licenses. The water right system is pluralistic, simultaneously recognizing a variety of doctrines to uphold water rights. Farmers holding **seniority rights** to water may receive priority in the use of water rights and may obtain water at much lower prices, thereby allowing inefficient use of water. Newer mechanisms that allow water to be sold to third parties will result in more efficient use of water.

WATER POLLUTION

Point source pollution An easily identifiable source of pollution such as discharges from wastewater treatment facilities, industrial, construction, or municipal discharges including sewer outfalls.

Non-point source pollution NPS has no single point of discharge. These sources are diffuse, sporadic, and difficult to trace, and thus more difficult to regulate through a permit process. Examples include runoff from agricultural, urban areas, timber operations, and mine drainage.

Federal Safe Drinking Water Act (SDWA) (1974) This act, significantly amended in 1986 and 1996, directs the USEPA (US Environmental Protection Agency) to set national standards for drinking water quality.

MCL (maximum contaminant level) The maximum concentration of a contaminant that is allowed in public *drinking water* systems. The level is chosen that maximizes the health-risk reduction benefits at a cost that is justified by the benefits.

California Safe Drinking Water Act (1976) This act, amended in 1989, allows the setting and enforcing of federal and state drinking water standards.

California 2006 Clean Water Act 303(d) list This act requires development of a list of waters that do not meet water quality standards even after point sources of pollution have installed the minimum required levels of pollution control technology.

Impaired water body A water body is impaired if it fails to meet the water quality standards.

TMDL (total maximum daily load) Definition of how much of a specific pollutant a water body can tolerate and still meet relevant water quality standards.

AIR POLLUTION

24-hour PM (particulate matter) Particulate matter is classified into macro size, that between 2.5 microns (or micrometers) and 10 microns, and fine particulate matter, with size smaller than 2.5 microns. Fine particulate matter gets trapped in the lungs and is much more harmful than coarse matter. Fine particulate matter is measured in two different ways: annual average and short-term levels (24 hour), the latter being referred to as 24-hour PM. High levels in either of these two measures pose health risks.

Weighted average of high pollution days The American Lung Association has designed a system to compute a weighted average of high pollution days by assigning higher weights to days with levels significantly above the desired levels and lower weights to days with low levels of pollution.

Standards for ozone pollution National standard: 75 ppm (parts per million) measured over 8 hours; California standard: 70 ppm.

Standards for particle pollution (24-hour PM) National Standard: 35 micro-grams/cubic meter; California Standard: 12 micor-grams/cubic meter.

Clean Air Act (1963) The US Congress passed the nation's landmark public health law, known as the Clean Air Act, about 40 years ago.

Ozone The ozone layer found in the upper atmosphere (the stratosphere) is beneficial because it shields us from much of the sun's ultraviolet radiation. However, ozone air pollution at ground level, where we breathe it in, is harmful.

TAC (toxic air contaminants) The most prevalent ten TACs are: acetaldehyde, benzene, butadiene, carbon tetrachloride, hexavalent chromium, para-dichlorobenzene, formaldehyde, methyl chloride, perchloroethylene, and diesel. Unfortunately, diesel is currently not monitored, although it has a higher health risk than the other nine TACs combined.

Meteorology's role in air pollution Highest ozone concentrations occur on hot and sunny days with light breezes or calm air. In some areas, wind movements from one region to another create high ozone levels. Particle pollution can be caused by strong winds that lift dust into air or can also be caused by cool and humid air that allows a build-up of secondary particulate matter in the atmosphere.

Air basins California is divided into 15 air basins on the basis of similar meteorological and geographical conditions. Air pollutants such as ozone and particulate matter, as well as their precursors, move freely across air basins, however.

Non-attainment designation A region has a non-attainment designation if the region does not meet the standards. As of 2007, 93% of California has non-attainment status for both ozone and particle pollution based on national standards and 99% non-attainment status based on state standards.

Sources of emissions Stationary sources include fuel combustion, waste disposal, cleaning and surface coatings, petroleum production, and industrial processes. Area-wide sources include pesticides and farming operations, asphalt paving, and residential fuel combustion, dust, fires, cooking. On-road mobile sources include transportation on road. Other mobile sources include aircrafts, trains, ocean vehicles, off-road recreational vehicles, and lawn, garden, farming equipment.

CARBON EMISSIONS

Greenhouse gases Following Kyoto universal standards, the six greenhouse gases are: carbon dioxide (CO_2), methane (CH_4), nitrous oxide (N_2O), sulfur hexafluoride (SF_6), hydrofluorocarbons (HFCs), and perfluorocarbons (PFCs). These gases absorb infrared radiation, directly impacting the atmosphere's capability to trap heat. The first three are emitted naturally or through the combustion of fossil fuels. The last three are synthetically produced for industrial purposes.

CO_2 Carbon dioxide constituted 89% of gross emissions in California in 1990, followed by methane (6%) and nitrous oxide (4%).

MMT CO_2e Million Metric Ton of Carbon Dioxide Equivalent. Same amount of different greenhouse gases warm the atmosphere by different amounts. This equivalent measure is a universal standard to measure the warming potential of any greenhouse gas in terms of one million metric ton of CO_2.

GWP gases High GWP (global warming potential) gases occur mostly in refrigeration, air conditioning systems, fire suppression systems, and the production of insulating foam.

K–12 (pronounced "k twelve", "k through twelve", or "k to twelve") is a designation for the sum of primary and secondary education. It is used in the USA, Canada, the Philippines, and Australia.

INEQUALITY & SOCIAL DIVIDES

GDP (PPP) Gross Domestic Product (Purchasing Power Parity). GDP is the value of all goods and services produced within a nation in a given year. A nation's GDP at purchasing power parity exchange rates is the sum value of all goods and services produced in the country valued at prices prevailing in the USA in the year noted.

High Net Worth Individuals Those having investable assets of $1 million or more, excluding primary residence, collectibles, consumables, and consumer durables.

Gini coefficient Gini coefficient is commonly used as a measure of inequality of income and wealth. It is the ratio of the area that lies between the diagonal line or the line of equality (45 degrees) and the income or wealth distribution curve divided by the total area under the line of equality. A Gini coefficient of zero expresses perfect equality. A Gini coefficient of 100 expresses maximal inequality. The range of Gini coefficients for all countries typically varies between 23 and 70.

Sources

CHAPTER 1: LAND & PEOPLE

18–19 LAND & NATURE
SAN ANDREAS FAULT SYSTEM
Map modified from Schultz, SS and Wallace, RA, 1997. Science for a changing world. geomaps.wr.usgs.gov

EARTHQUAKES
California Earthquake Map Collection. Isoseismal Maps for Selected California Earthquakes. geology.com

Historic Earthquakes in the United States and Its Territories. earthquake.usgs.gov

Southern California Earthquake Data Center. www.data.scec.org

VEGETATION
Based on vegetation map by Jeremiah Easter and Wildlife Habitats map produced as part of The California GAP Analysis Project.

20–21 PARKS & PUBLIC LANDS
FOUNDING OF CALIFORNIA'S STATE PARKS
California State Park System Statistical Report 2009/10. California State Parks, Statewide Planning Unit. www.parks.ca.gov

CALIFORNIA'S PUBLIC LANDS
National Parks: Eureka Cartography www.maps-eureka.com

California Public Lands. BLM, 2008. www.blm.gov

State Parks: www.parks.ca.gov

Marine sanctuaries and reserves: California State Marine Protected Areas. www.californiampas.org

22–23 COLONIALISM & NATIVE CALIFORNIANS
An Introduction to California's Native people. www.cabrillo.edu

Selby, WA. Rediscovering the Golden State. John Wiley & Sons, 2006.

CALIFORNIA EMERGING FROM MEXICO
US Territorial Map 1840. xroads.virginia.edu

NATIVE CALIFORNIANS
Selby, op cit.

US Census data 1950, 2010. www.census.gov

POPULATION OF NATIVE AMERICANS
Cook, Sherburne F. The Population of the California Indians: 1769-1970. University of California Press, 1976.

US Census data 1950 onwards. www.census.gov

24–25 POPULATION
Bohn, S. New patterns of Immigrant Settlement in California. Public Policy Institute of California, July 2009. www.ppic.org

Public Policy Institute of California. Just the Facts series of briefings: California's Future Population (September 2008); California's Inland Empire: 2015 (April 2008); Immigrants in California (April 2011); Are the rich leaving California? (July 2009). www.ppic.org

RACE/ETHNICITY AND ORIGIN
2010 Census Briefs, Overview of Race and Hispanic Origin: 2010, Table 2, March 2011. United States Census Bureau. www.census.gov

IMMIGRATION TRENDS
US Historical Immigration Trends. MPI Data Hub. www.migrationinformation.org

State of California Total Population, 1850 to 2010. Department of Finance. www.dof.ca.gov

POPULATION DENSITY AND CHANGE
Selected Decennial Census Population and Housing Counts. www.census.gov

AGE DISTRIBUTION
DP-1: Profile of General Population and Housing Characteristics: 2010. www.census.gov

26–27 MIGRATION
Bohn, S. New patterns of Immigrant Settlement in California. Public Policy Institute of California, July 2009. www.ppic.org

Digital History, Landmarks in Immigration History. www.digitalhistory.uh.edu

Meeker, M. Introduction to We are California Project. www.weareca.org

Public Policy Institute of California. Just the Facts briefing: Immigrants in California, April 2011. www.ppic.org

AGE PROFILE
ECONOMIC CHARACTERISTICS
EDUCATIONAL CHARACTERISTICS
US Census Bureau, American Community Survey, 2011. www.census.gov

HISTORICAL GROWTH
Bohn, 2009, op cit.

Historical Census Statistics on the Foreign-Born Population of the United States: 1850-2000. www.census.gov

Historical Population Trends, State of California Total Population, 1850 to 2010. www.dof.ca.gov

FOREIGN-BORN POPULATION
Migration Policy Institute Data Hub. www.migrationinformation.org

CALIFORNIA'S IMMIGRANT POPULATION
PPIC, April 2011, op. cit.

28–29 UNAUTHORIZED IMMIGRATION
CALIFORNIA'S SHARE;
UNAUTHORIZED IMMIGRANTS
Hill, LE, Johnson, HP. Unauthorized Immigrants in California: Estimates for Counties. PPIC, July 2011, p7. www.ppic.org

OCCUPATIONS DEPENDENT ON IMMIGRATION
Passel, JS, Cohn, D. A Portrait of Unauthorized Immigrants in the United States. Pew Hispanic Research Center, April, 2009, p31. www.pewhispanic.org

COUNTRY OF ORIGIN
Hoefer, M, Rytina, N, Baker, B. Estimates of the Unauthorized Immigrant Population Residing in the United States: January 2011. www.dhs.gov

CHAPTER 2: POLITICS, GOVERNANCE, & POWER

32–33 GOVERNMENT & POLITICS
CALIFORNIA'S VOTERS
RACIAL/ETHNIC BREAKDOWN
California's likely voters, PPIC, Aug 2012. www.ppic.org

Improving California's democracy, PPIC, Oct 2012. www.ppic.org

STATE AND LOCAL GOVERNMENT EMPLOYEES
Government employment and payroll. www.census.gov/govs/apes

VOTING PATTERN
United States presidential election in California, 2012. Statement of Vote, November 6, 2010. pp. 19-21. www.sos.ca.gov

CONTROL OF CALIFORNIA'S SENATE AND ASSEMBLY
Political party strength in California. en.wikipedia.org

California State Legislature, 2013-13 Sessions. en.wikipedia.org

34–35 BUDGET & TAXATION
Oliff, P, Mai, C, Palacios, V. States Continue to Feel Recession Impact. Center on Budget and Policy Priorities, June 27, 2012. www.cbpp.org/cms

State Expenditure Report 2010. National Association of State Budget Officers, December 2011. www.nasbo.org

Total California State Tax per Capita. Department of Finance. CA Statistical Abstract. www.dof.ca.gov

CALIFORNIA'S DEBT OBLIGATIONS
California Budget Information. Chart K-3. California's Department of Finance. www.dof.ca.gov.

REVENUE VOLATILITY
California's Fiscal Outlook, 1995-2011. Legislative Analyst Office. www.lao.ca.gov

OPERATING BUDGET AND SHORTFALLS
General Fund History: Revenues and Transfers vs. Expenditures, Chart A-1. California's Department of Finance. www.dof.ca.gov/budgeting

CALIFORNIA'S TAX BURDEN
STATE AND LOCAL TAXES
State and Local Tax Revenue as a Percentage of Personal Income. Tax Policy Center, December 16, 2011. www.taxpolicycenter.org

Comparative State and Local Taxes, 2009. Department of Revenue, Washington State. dor.wa.gov

36–37 GOVERNMENT FINANCES
GENERAL REVENUE
GENERAL EXPENDITURE
2010 Annual Surveys of State and Local Government Finances. US Census Bureau. www.census.gov

COMPARISON OF TAX REVENUE SOURCES
State and Local Government Finances. US Census Bureau. www.census.gov

STATE DEBT
Financial Data. Fiscal Years 2010-11 and 2011-12. p8. California State Treasurer's Office. www.treasurer.ca.gov

38–39 MILITARY POWER
California Historic and Military Buildings and Structures Inventory, vols I-IV, www.denix.osd.mil

Military Base Closures: the Impact on California Communities, RB-7511. www.rand.org

DEFENSE PERSONNEL
Statistical Information Analysis Division, Work Force Publications. Siadapp.dmdc.osd.mil

Distribution of Personnel by State and by Selected Locations, 2009 (M02 Tables). www.census.gov

CALIFORNIA'S SHARE OF MILITARY RESOURCES
Distribution of Personnel by State and by Selected Locations, 1994-2009 (M02 Tables). www.census.gov

Expenditure: Consolidated Federal Funds Report (1981-2011), US Census Bureau. www.census.gov

Personnel: Statistical Information Analysis Division, Work Force Publications. Siadapp.dmdc.osd.mil

MILITARY INSTALLATIONS
Base Structure Report 2011, Department of Defense. www.acq.osd.mil

The Report of the California Council on Base Support and Retention. California: The Key to Transforming America's Military. April 7, 2005, p68.

40–41 CRIME & INCARCERATION
Characteristics of Inmate Population Report Archive, December 2010. California Department of Corrections and Rehabilitation (CDCR). Web. April 8, 2012. www.cdcr.ca.gov

Crime Rates by State, US Census Bureau, 2012. www.census.com

Historical Trends Report Archive, California Department of Corrections and Rehabilitation (CDCR). April 8, 2012. www.cdcr.ca.gov

Population Reports, California Department of Corrections and Rehabilitation (CDCR) Office of Research, March 31, 2012. www.cdcr.ca.gov

Prisoners in 2010, US Department of Justice Bureau of Justice Statistics, December 2011.

Steady Climb, State Corrections Spending in California, September 2011. California Budget Project. www.cbp.org

RACIAL DISPARITY; DRUG FELONS
Historical Trends Report Archive, op. cit.

Characteristics of Inmate Population Report Archive December 2010, op. cit.

CRIME AND PUNISHMENT
Crime Rates by State, US Census Bureau. www.census.gov

Guerino, P, Harrison, PM, Sabol, WJ. *Prisoners in 2010.* US Department of Justice Bureau of Justice Statistics, December 2011, Appendix Table 9. bjs.ojp.usdoj.gov (Imprisonment includes those in state and county jails, and prisoners sentenced for one year or more.)

PROPERTY AND VIOLENT CRIMES
Harris KD, Attorney General. *Crime in California 2012.* California Department of Justice. oag.ca.gov

STATE PRISON OVERCROWDING
Historical Trends Report Archive, op. cit.
Population Reports, op. cit.

"Indeed, it is an uncontested fact..."
Findings of Fact and Conclusions of Law Re Appointment of Receiver. Plata/Coleman v. Schwarzenegger. United States District Court Northern District of California, 2011. Web. 09 Apr. 2012. www.cand.uscourts.gov

FUNDING
Steady Climb, State Corrections Spending in California, op. cit.

CAPITAL PUNISHMENT IN CALIFORNIA
History of Capital Punishment in California. www.cdcr.ca.gov

CHAPTER 3: ECONOMY & INDUSTRY

44–45 ECONOMIC GROWTH
TOP ECONOMIES
GDP GROWTH RATE
The World Bank. databank.worldbank.org
US Department of Commerce. www.bea.gov

CALIFORNIA: THE ECONOMIC ENGINE OF AMERICA; CALIFORNIA'S ECONOMY; MANUFACTURING
US Department of Commerce. www.bea.gov

46–47 WORKFORCE
California Statistical Abstract, California Department of Finance. www.dof.ca.gov

Employment Development Department of the State of California. www.labormarketinfo.edd.ca.gov

Employment Status of the Population, US Bureau of Labor Statistics. www.bls.gov

Milkman, R, Rooks, D. California Union Membership: A Turn-of-the-Century Portrait. www.ruthmilkman.info

AVERAGE WEEKLY WAGE
Employment and Wages Online, 2011. www.bls.gov

UNION MEMBERSHIP
Union Membership in California, 2011. www.bls.gov

LABOR FORCE GROWTH
Civilian Labor Force, Employment, and Unemployment, California Statistical Abstract, Table C-1, www.dof.ca.gov

Labor Force and Unemployment Data. www.labormarketinfo.edd.ca.gov

LABOR FORCE
HOW CALIFORNIA'S WAGES COMPARE
www.labormarketinfo.edd.ca.gov.
www.bls.gov

OCCUPATIONS WITH MOST JOB OPENINGS
Projections of Employment. www.labormarketinfo.edd.ca.gov.

48–49 BUSINESS & FINANCE
START-UPS
Fairlie, RW. *Kauffman Index of Entrepreneurial Activity 1996–2011.* Kauffman, March 2012. Table 4, p20.

GLOBAL REACH
Apple Inc. Supplier List 2013. images.apple.com

ChinaFile www.chinafile.com

BIG BUSINESS
Fortune 500 for California: money.cnn.com

BANKING DEPOSITS
Census Table 1181. FDIC-Insured Financial Institutions — Number of Offices and Deposits by State: 2009: www.census.gov

50–51 AGRIBUSINESS
MAJOR CALIFORNIAN CROPS
California Agricultural Statistics. 2011 Crop Year. USDA. p5. www.nass.usda.gov/ca

MAJOR DESTINATIONS OF AGRICULTURAL EXPORTS
University of California Agricultural Issues Center. Estimating California's Agricultural Exports. 2010 California Agricultural Export Data, Table 4. aic.ucdavis.edu/pub/exports.html

AGRIBUSINESS HEARTLAND
Agricultural employment in California. Agricultural Bulletin. 2011 map. www.labormarketinfo.edd.ca.gov [Accessed March 2013]

Food manufacturing production: Food Manufacturing in California. Northern California Center of Excellence and the Office of Economic Development at Cerritos College. 2010, p7. www.coeccc.net

Value of agricultural production: California County Agricultural Commissioners' Reports 2011, p4. 2011. [Figures without timber, reduced by a factor of .845 to conform with USDA method of calculating sales.] www.nass.usda.gov/ca

AGRICULTURAL POWERHOUSE
U.S. and State Farm Income and Wealth Statistics. Ranking of states for total net farm income, 2011. www.nass.usda.gov

52–53 TECHNOLOGY
PATENTS GRANTED WORLDWIDE
SHARE OF US PATENTS
US Patent and Trademark Office. Patents by country, state, and year - Utility patents. December 2011. www.uspto.gov

LABOR PRODUCTIVITY
Rhode, PW. *The Evolution of California Manufacturing.* Public Policy Institute of California, 2001. Table 7.1. www.ppic.org

HIGH-TECH EMPLOYMENT
Technology Works: High-Tech employment and wages in the United States. A Bay Area Council Economic Institute Report commissioned by Engine Advocacy. December 2012. www.bayareacouncil.org

VENTURE CAPITAL
Investments by Region. Silicon Valley, Q4 2012. Money Tree Report. www.pwcmoneytree.com

CHAPTER 4: URBAN AREAS

56–57 CITIES & METRO AREAS

POPULATION AND GDP
Statista. GDP of the San Francisco Bay Area. www.statista.com [Accessed Feb 20, 2013]

United States Census Bureau. Table 1. Annual Estimates of the Population of Metropolitan and Micropolitan Statistical Areas. www.census.gov [Accessed March 25, 2013]

CROSS-SECTION OF URBAN DENSITY
POPULATION DENSITY
Patterns of Metropolitan and Micropolitan Population Change: 2000 to 2010. 2010 Census Briefs. March 2011. C2010BR-01. www.census.gov

MAJOR METROPOLITAN AREAS
Table 1. Annual Estimates of the Population of Metropolitan and Micropolitan Statistical Areas. www.census.gov [Accessed March 25, 2013]

58–59 THE BAY AREA

TOP MILLIONAIRE METRO AREAS
Capgemini Releases the 2011 U.S. Metro Wealth Index, Business Wire, July 12, 2011. www.businesswire.com

EDUCATIONAL ATTAINMENT
US Census Bureau, American Community Survey, 2010 1-Year Estimates. Table S. 1501. www.census.gov

URBAN GROWTH IN THE BAY AREA
GreenInfo Network. www.greeninfo.org/about.php

INCOME IN SAN FRANCISCO
US Census Bureau. www.census.gov

60–61 GREATER LOS ANGELES

UP AND OUT
Historical Census Populations of Counties and Incorporated Cities in California, 1850–2010. www.dof.ca.gov

CITIES WITHIN A CITY
US Census of Population, 2010. www.census.gov

MAJOR EMPLOYMENT SECTORS
EED, Labor Market Info Division March 2011.

62–63 REAL ESTATE

THE NATION'S PRICIEST HOUSES
Table 978. Median Sales Price of One-Family Homes by Selected Metropolitan Areas. www.census.gov

NEW CONSTRUCTION
Construction Industry Research Board, (Security Pacific through 1986), seasonally adjusted by the CA Dept. of Finance.

HOUSE PRICES
Federal Housing Finance Agency House Price Index. www.fhfa.gov

NEW HOUSING STARTS IN GREATER BAY AREA
FORECLOSURES
RUBBLE OF THE BUBBLE
Rand California. Business and Economic Statistics. ca.rand.org

64–65 HIGHWAYS & TRANSPORTATION

MODE OF TRAVEL
Freemark, Y, Transit Mode Share Trends Looking Steady; Rail appears to encourage non-automobile commutes. *The Transport Politic.* October 13, 2010. Table: Mode Share of Nation's Largest Metropolitan Areas 2009. www.thetransportpolitic.com

BAY AREA COMMUTER FLOWS
Commuter Forecasts for the San Francisco Bay Area: 1990-2030. Based on ABAG Projections 2003 and Census 2000: Data Summary (May 2004). www.mtc.ca.gov

CALIFORNIA'S TRANSPORT INFRASTRUCTURE
Fourth Quarter 2010 US Airport Traffic Snapshot, The 175 Top Passenger O&D Airports Ranked By Passengers. Prepared By Boyd Group International Inc. www.AviationPlanning.com

US SEAPORTS
Table 1087. Top US Ports by Container Traffic: 2009. www.census.gov

AUTOMOBILES PER CAPITA
14% of all US vehicles...
Office of Highway Policy Information. Highway Statistics 2010. Table MV-1. www.fhwa.dot.gov

CHAPTER 5 WATER & ENERGY

68–69 WATER SUPPLY

Bulletin 160-98, The California Water Plan Update, 1998. California Department of Water Resources. www.waterplan.water.ca.gov

California Department of Water Resources Plan Update 2009. California Department of Water Resources. www.waterplan.water.ca.gov

Dowall, D, Washington, J. *Making Room for the Future: Rebuilding California's Infrastructure.* Public Policy Institute of California, 2003. www.ppic.org

Hanak, E et al. *Managing California's Water: From Conflict to Reconciliation.* Public Policy Institute of California, 2011. www.ppic.org

Hanak, E, Baldassare, M. *California 2025: Taking on the Future.* Public Policy Institute of California, 2005. www.ppic.org

Levee Failures in the Sacramento-San Joaquin River Delta. DWR Poster prepared in collaboration with URS Corporation, 2007. www.water.ca.gov

OUTFLOW AND USE
Delta Vision Blue Ribbon Task Force Report, 2008. State of California Water Resources Agency. deltavision.ca.gov

FLUCTUATION BETWEEN WET AND DRY YEARS
Department of Water Resources. WSIHIST. cdec.water.ca.gov/cgi-progs/iodir/WSIHIST

WATER STORAGE AND TRANSFER SYSTEM
California Water Plan Update 2009, Volume 1, Chapter 4 California Water Today, p6. California Department of Water Resources. www.waterplan.water.ca.gov

PRECIPITATION
nationalatlas.gov

70–72 WATER USE

As for **Water Supply** above.

WATER USE
Hanak et al, 2011, op. cit.

PRODUCTIVITY OF WATER USE IN FARM CROPS
Hanak et al. 2011, op. cit. p92.

TOTAL WATER USE
PER CAPITA WATER USE
Hanak et al. 2011, op. cit. pp.89-90.

WATER AVAILABILITY AND USE
California Groundwater Update Bulletin 118-2003. Department of Water Resources. www.water.ca.gov

72–73 ENERGY: FOSSIL FUELS

California Energy Balance Update and Decomposition Analysis for the Industry and Building Sectors. Lawrence Berkeley National Lab, December 2010. uc-ciee.org

California Energy Commission, Integrated Energy Policy Report, 2007, CEC-100-2007-008-CMF. www.energy.ca.gov

California Energy Commission, Integrated Energy Policy Report, 2011, CEC-100-2011-001-CMF US Energy Information Administration. www.eia.gov

Development of Energy Balances for the State of California. Lawrence Berkeley National Lab, June 2005, CEC-500-2005-068. www.energy.ca.gov

COMPARATIVE ENERGY CONSUMPTION
US Energy Information Administration. www.eia.gov
US Energy Information Administration, Table 31. Energy Consumption Overview. www.eia.gov

CALIFORNIA'S PER CAPITA ENERGY CONSUMPTION
Table CT2. Primary Energy Consumption Estimates, Selected Years, 1960-2010, California. www.eia.gov

WHAT ENERGY IS USED FOR
ENERGY SUPPLY
ENERGY USE
FOSSIL FUEL PRODUCTION AND RISING IMPORTS
California Energy Balance Update and Decomposition Analysis for the Industry and Building Sectors. Lawrence Berkeley National Lab, December 2010. uc-ciee.org

74–75 ENERGY: ELECTRICITY

As for **Energy: Fossil Fuel**, above

PER CAPITA ELECTRICITY CONSUMPTION
California Energy Commission, 2008 Net System Power Report, p 5. www.energy.ca.gov

ELECTRICITY CONSUMPTION
ELECTRICITY CONSUMPTION TRENDS
The California Energy Commission. Energy Almanac. energyalmanac.ca.gov
Price data downloaded from www.eia.gov

CHANGE IN ENERGY EFFICIENCY
California Energy Balance Update and Decomposition Analysis for the Industry and Building Sectors. Lawrence Berkeley National Lab, December 2010. uc-ciee.org

76–77 Renewable Energy
CALIFORNIA TAKES THE LEAD
Renewable Energy Annual 2008, August 2010, Table 1.20, p32. US Energy Information Administration. ftp.eia.doe.gov

IN-STATE ELECTRICITY GENERATION
California Energy Commission. Energy Almanac. Total Electricity System Power energyalmanac.ca.gov

RENEWABLE ELECTRICITY CAPACITY
California Energy Commission, Renewable Power in California: Status and Issues, August 2011, CEC-150-2011-002, Table A-1 (Appendix A) for capacity. www.energy.ca.gov
California Energy Commission. Energy Almanac. Database of Power Plants in California. energyalmanac.ca.gov

CHAPTER 6 ENVIRONMENT
80–81 Climate Change
Moser, S, et al. The future is now: An Update on Climate Change Science Impacts and Response Options for California. California Energy Commission Report, September 2008 (CEC-500-2008-077), May 2009 (CDC-500-2008-071). www.energy.ca.gov
Pittiglio et al. Annual Minimum and Maximum Temperature Anomalies in California by Climatic Region, 1920-2003. www.energy.ca.gov
Thorne, JH. Dynamics of Sierra Nevada Conifer Loss Under Climate Change. Contract with California Energy Commission: 500-07-004, 2008.

WINTER CHILL HOURS
Baldocchi and Wong. Data derived from the California Climate Archive, cited in Moser et al, 2008, p18.

Potential loss of over $3.3...
Moser et al, p19.

SEA-LEVEL RISE
Moser et al, op. cit. Short report, p25.

REGIONAL TEMPERATURE CHANGE
California Energy Commission. California Building Climate Zone Map. www.energy.ca.gov
Pittiglio et al, op. cit.

WINTER FREEZE LINE
Moser et al, op. cit., p22.

TEMPERATURE INCREASE
Moser et al, op. cit., p10.

82–83 Carbon Emissions
Bedsworth, L. Climate Change Challenges: Vehicle Emissions and Public Health in California, Public Policy Institute of California, March 2010.

Climate Change Scoping Plan, December 2008, California Air Resources Board. www.arb.ca.gov
Stanton, E, et al, Greenhouse Gases and the American Lifestyle: Understanding Interstate Differences in Emissions. Ecotrust, May 2009. www.e3network.org

COMPARATIVE EMISSIONS
World Resources Institute, cait.wri.org [Accessed March 2012]
Climate Change Scoping Plan, op. cit.

TRENDS IN GHG EMISSIONS
MAJOR INDUSTRIAL SOURCES OF CARBON EMISSIONS
California Air Resources Board, California Greenhouse Gas Inventory for 2000-2008 and 1990-2004. www.arb.ca.gov

VEHICLE MILES TRAVELED
US Department of Transportation, Highway Statistics Publications, 1992-2009. www.fhwa.dot.gov

GREENHOUSE GAS EMISSIONS
Climate Change Scoping Plan, op. cit., p13.

84–85 Air Pollution
EMISSIONS TRENDS
California Air Resources Board, The California Almanac of Emissions and Air Quality, 2009, www.arb.ca.gov

IMPACT ON HEALTH
HIGH POLLUTION DAYS
TOP TEN MOST POLLUTED AREAS
American Lung Association, State of the Air, 2011. www.stateoftheair.org

86–87 Water Pollution
Department of Water Resources Plan Update 2009. www.waterplan.water.ca.gov
EPA finalizes California's list of Polluted Waters. yosemite.epa.gov [Accessed 10/11/2011]
Hanak et al, Managing California's Water: From Conflict to Reconciliation. Public Policy Institute of California, 2011. www.ppic.org
REACH. (Registration, Evaluation, Authorisation and Restriction of Chemical substances) ec.europa.eu

SOURCES OF POLLUTION AND DISRUPTION BY HUMAN ACTIVITY
EPA, California Assessment Data for 2004. L17-N26, Impaired Lakes, Reservoirs, and Ponds. iaspub.epa.gov

IMPAIRED WATER
EPA, California Assessment Data for 2004. Individual Designated Use Support California Lakes, Reservoirs, and Ponds. iaspub.epa.gov

WATER QUALITY HOT SPOTS
Anderson, BS et al, Integrated assessment of the impacts of agricultural drainwater in the Salinas River (California, USA). Environmental Pollution 124 (2003) 523–532.
Beckon, WN, Henderson, JD, Maurer, TC, Schwarzbach, SE. Biological Effects of the Reopening of the San Luis Drain (Grasslands Bypass Project) to Carry Subsurface Irrigation Drainwater. USFWS, Div. of Env. Contaminants, Sacramento, CA., Sept. 1997.
Environmental Setting of the San Joaquin–Tulare Basins, California. Water Resources Investigations Report 97-4205. National

Water-Quality Assessment Program. Sacramento, 1998.
Hanak et al, op. cit., 2011. p85.
Introduction to the Sacramento River Basin. U.S. Geological Survey Circular 1215. U.S. Geological Survey. 2005-09-01. Retrieved 2010-08-31

NATIVE CALIFORNIAN FISH
Hanak et al, op. cit., p6.

CHAPTER 7 HEALTH & EDUCATION
90–91 Healthcare: Quality & Outcomes
HEALTH DISPARITIES
Johnson, HP and Hayes, JM. The Demographics of Mortality in California. PPIC, May 2004.
Lee, H and McConville, S. Death in the Golden State. PPIC, August 2007.

HEALTHCARE QUALITY
2011 Snapshots. National Healthcare Quality Report, 2011. p12, Figure H.8, Table H.4. statesnapshots.ahrq.gov

HEALTH OUTCOMES
HEALTH FACTORS
County Rankings and Roadmaps: California Summary Report, 2012. University of Wisconsin Population Health Institute. www.countyhealthrankings.org

92–93 Healthcare: Cost & Access
HEALTHCARE SPENDING
INCREASING HEALTHCARE SPENDING
California Health Care Foundation. California Health Care Almanac, Health Care Costs 101: California Addendum, May 2012. Appendix A, p30. www.chcf.org

HEALTH INSURANCE STATUS
US Census, Current Population Survey. www.census.gov

HEALTH INSURANCE COVERAGE IN CALIFORNIA
CHARACTERISTICS OF UNINSURED
Fronstin, P. California's Uninsured: Treading Water. Employee Benefit Research Institute, December 2012. California Health Care Foundation. California Health Care Almanac. www.chcf.org

94–95 Pre-K Education
Cannon, JS, Jacknowitz, A and Karoly, Lynn A. Preschool and School Readiness. PPIC, May 2012. www.ppic.org
ChildCare Aware of America, Parents and the High Cost of Child Care. 2012. www.naccrra.org
Karoly, Lynn A. The Use of Early Care and Education by California Families. Rand Corporation, 2012. www.rand.org
The National Institute for Early Education Research, The State of Preschool 2011. nieer.org

CALIFORNIA PRE-K PROVISION
Karoly, 2012, op. cit.

PRE-K EDUCATION
Kids Count. datacenter.kidscount.org

The State of Preschool 2011, Table 5, p17. nieer.org

Parents and the High Cost of Child Care. 2012. Appendix I, Table 36. www.naccrra.org

ACCESS TO PRESCHOOL
California County Scorecard, 2012, Indicator 5. Children Now. scorecard.childrennow.org

ACCESS TO CENTER-BASED CARE
Cannon et al, 2012, op. cit.

96–97 K–12 EDUCATION
PATHWAY TO COLLEGE
California Educational Opportunity Report, 2011, UCLA/IDEA. idea.gseis.ucla.edu

VARIATION IN FUNDING PER PUPIL
California Watch, California School District Spending and Test Scores, June 2, 2011. schoolspending.apps.cironline.org

Federal Education Budget Project, New America Foundation. febp.newamerica.net/k12/

EXPENDITURE PER PUPIL
Quality Counts, *Edweek*, January 10, 2013. www.edweek.org

STUDENT–TEACHER RATIO
Public Elementary and Secondary School Student Enrollment and Staff Counts from the Common Core of Data: School Year 2010-11, National Center for Educational Statistics, Table 4. nces.ed.gov

98–99 HIGHER EDUCATION
California Postsecondary Education Commission. www.cpec.ca.gov

Fiscal Profiles, 2010, California Postsecondary Education Commission, December 2010. www.cpec.ca.gov

Johnson, H. *California Workforce: Planning for a better future*. PPIC, Jan 2013. www.ppic.org

Johnson, H. *Defunding Higher Education*: *What are the effect on college enrollment?* PPIC, May 2012. www.ppic.org

Kelly, Patrick. *Closing the College Attainment Gap between the US and Most Educated Countries, and the Contributions to be made by the States*. National Center for Higher Education Management System, April 2010. www.nchems.org

National Center for Educational Statistics. www.nces.ed.gov

Trends in College Spending 1999-2009, A report of the Delta Cost Project. www.deltacostproject

GOVERNMENT FUNDING FOR HIGHER EDUCATION
Postsecondary Education Commission. Fiscal Snapshots. www.cpec.ca.gov

CHANGING PRIORITIES
Public Higher Education Funding Graphs. www.cpec.ca.gov

Steady Climb, State Corrections Spending in California, September 2011. www.cbp.org

STUDENT FEE INCREASE
Resident Undergraduate Fees Options [Accessed Feb 11, 2012] www.cpec.ca.gov

TUITION FEE BURDEN
Fiscal Profiles, op. cit.

COLLEGE DEGREE COMPARISON
New State-by-State College Attainment Numbers. US Department of Education, July 12, 2012. www.ed.gov

ECONOMIC VALUE OF HIGHER EDUCATION
Postsecondary Education Value - Median Income vs. Unemployment. www.cpec.ca.gov

CHAPTER 8 INEQUALITY & SOCIAL DIVIDES
Hanauer, N. Who are the Job Creators? Speech and slideshow originally presented as a TED talk on March 1, 2012, hosted on: Here Is the Full Inequality Speech and Slideshow That Was Too Hot for TED. May 17, 2012. www.theatlantic.com

Lardner, J, Smith D (editors). *Inequality Matters: The growing economic divide in America and its poisonous Consequences*. The New Press, 2007.

Rohde, D. The Unequal State of America: Does income inequality matter? And how? Reuters, December 19, 2012. www.reuters.com

Sen, A. *Inequality Re-Examined*. Harvard University Press, 1992.

Therborn, G et al. *Inequalities of the World: New theoretical frameworks, multiple empirical approaches*. Verso, 2006.

Wilkinson, R. How economic inequality harms societies, July 2011, TED Talk. www.ted.com

Wilkinson, R, Pickett, K. *The Spirit Level. Why equality is better for everyone*. London: Allen Lane, 2009.

How does inequality matter, *The Economist*, Jan 21, 2011. www.economist.com

102–03 INCOME, WEALTH, & POVERTY
A Generation of Widening Inequality, California Budget Project, November 2011. www.cbp.org

California's Welfare Caseload, Public Policy Unit of California, February 2012.

Lindert, PH, Williamson JG. *American Incomes 1774-1860*. The National Bureau of Economic Research, September 2012. www.nber.org

Mishel, L, Bivens, J, Gould, E, Shierholz, H. *The State of Working America*. 12th Edition, 2012. stateofworkingamerica.org/

Taxing the Rich, *The Week*, November 4, 2011.

The Research Supplemental Poverty Measure: 2011, US Census Bureau, November 2012. www.census.gov

HOW CALIFORNIA COMPARES
Household Income for States: 2010 and 2011, US Census Bureau. www.census.gov

The World Factbook. Country Comparison: Distribution of Family Income – Gini Index. www.cia.gov

RISING CEO-TO-WORKER COMPENSATION RATIO
WIDENING GAP BETWEEN RICH AND POOR IN USA
Mishel, L et al. 2012

The wealthy are 288 times richer than you. September 11, 2012. money.cnn.com

INCREASING INCOME INEQUALITY IN CALIFORNIA
A Generation of Widening Inequality, op. cit.

POVERTY RATE
The Research Supplemental Poverty Measure. op. cit.

104–05 HUNGER & HOMELESSNESS
California Nutrition and Food Insecurity Profile 2010, California Food Policy Advocates, cfpa.net

Chaparro, MP et al. *Nearly Four Million Californians are Food Insecure*. UCLA Center for Health Policy Research, June 2012. healthpolicy.ucla.edu

Danielson, C, Klerman, JA. *California's Food Stamp Program*. Public Policy Institute of California, September 2011.

Greater Los Angeles Homeless Count Report 2009, Los Angeles Homeless Services Authority Commissioners. www.lahsa.org

Household Food Security in the US in 2011, US Department of Agriculture, September 2012. www.ers.usda.gov

Map the Meal Gap: Child Food Insecurity, Feeding America, 2011.

The 2012 Point-in-Time Estimates of Homelessness, US Department of Housing and Urban Development, 2012. www. onecpd.info

US HOMELESS
HOMELESS IN CALIFORNIA
The 2012 Point-in-Time Estimates of Homelessness, op. cit.

CHARACTERISTICS OF LOS ANGELES' HOMELESS
2009 Greater Los Angeles Homeless Count Report, op. cit.

VERY LOW FOOD SECURITY
Chaparro, MP et al, 2012.

POVERTY RATE
United States Department of Agriculture. County-level Data Sets. Percent of total population in poverty, 2011. [Accessed March 2013.]

HOUSEHOLDS WITH LOW FOOD SECURITY
Household Food Security in the US in 2011, op. cit.

106–07 RACE & ETHNICITY
POVERTY RATE
US Census Bureau, Table S1701. www.census.gov

BUSINESS EMPOWERMENT
California Women Business Leaders 2012-13, UC Davis Graduate School of Management. viewer.zmags.com

POLITICAL EMPOWERMENT
Alexandar, A. *Citizen Legislators or Political Musical Chairs: Term limits in California*. Center for Governmental Studies, 2011. policyarchive.org

MEDIAN WEALTH
Mishel, L et al. *The State of Working America*. 12th edition. Chapter 6 Wealth. Table 6.5. stateofworkingamerica.org

RACE IN LOS ANGELES
INCOME IN LOS ANGELES
www.census.gov

108–109 GENDER & SEXUAL ORIENTATION

CORPORATE BOARD MEMBERS
California Women Business Leaders 2012-13. UC Davis Graduate School of Management. p10. viewer.zmags.com

GENDER GAP IN USA
The Global Gender Gap Report 2012, World Economic Forum. www3.weforum.org

WOMEN IN CALIFORNIA STATE LEGISLATURE
California Legislative Women's Caucus. Membership. womenscaucus.legislature.ca.gov

MEDIAN WAGES
US Census Bureau, 2011 ACS 3-year estimates, Tables B20017 to Tables B20017I, Median Earnings. www.census.gov

HATE CRIMES IN CALIFORNIA
Hate Crime Statistics 2011, FBI. www.fbi.gov

VIEWS ON GAY MARRIAGE
Egan PJ, Sherrill K. California's Proposition 8: What happened and what does the future hold? January 2009. www.thetaskforce.org

110–11 YOUTH & OLD AGE

Bohn, Sarah. *Child Poverty in California. Just the Facts.* Public Policy Institute of California, December 2011. www.ppic.org

California Children with Special Health Care Needs. Fact Sheet, November 2012. Lucile Packard Foundation for Children's Health. cshcn.wpengine.netdna-cdn.com

California Health Care Almanac, California's Uninsured, December 2011. California HealthCare Foundation. www.chcf.org

California Healthy Kids Survey, Student Well-being in California, 2009-11: Statewide Results. San Francisco: WestEd Health and Human Development Program for the California Department of Education. chks. wested.org

Children with Special Healthcare Needs. A Profile of Key Issues in California. Child and Adolescent Health Measurement Initiative. November 2010. www.lpfch.org/ specialneeds/

Even Critics of Safety Net Increasingly Depend on It. *New York Times*, February 9, 2012. www.nytimes.com

Kids Count. www.kidsdata.org/

Map the Meal Gap: Child Food Insecurity 2012. Feeding America. feedingamerica.org

Pearce, Dana. *Overlooked and Undercounted 2009. Struggling to make ends meet in California.* School of Social Work, University of Washington, 2009. www.insightcced.org

Wallace, Steven P, et al. *Characteristics of Adults age 65 and older with Incomes Below the 2007 Elder Economic Security Standard™ Index, California.* UCLA Center for Health Policy Research, February 2009. healthpolicy.ucla.edu

AGE DISTRIBUTION
US Census Bureau. www.census.gov

CHILDREN IN NEED
California Health Care Almanac, California's Uninsured, December 2011, op. cit.

California Children with Special Health Care Needs. Fact Sheet, November 2012, op. cit.

Bohn, Sarah, op. cit. 2011.

Map the Meal Gap: Child Food Insecurity 2012, op. cit.

Children with Special Healthcare Needs. November 2010, op. cit.

ECONOMICALLY INSECURE ELDERS
Wallace, Steven P, et al, 2007, op. cit.

YOUNG PEOPLE AT RISK
California Healthy Kids Survey, 2009-11, op. cit.

Child and Youth Safety. California. www.kidsdata.org

GOVERNMENT BENEFITS
The Geography of Government Benefits. *New York Times*, February 11, 2012 www.nytimes.com

ECONOMIC INSECURITY
Pearce, Dana, op. cit. Table B-19, pp89-90.

CHAPTER 9 CHALLENGES AHEAD

California Dreaming: Imagining New Futures for the State. Institute of Future, 2010. www.ittf.org

Grunwald, M. Why California is still America's Future. *Time Magazine*, Oct 23, 2009. www.time.com

McWilliams, C, Lapham, LH. *California: The Great Exception.* University of California Press, 1999.

Price, SD (editor). *1001 Greatest Things Ever Said About California.* The Lyons Press, 2007.

Schrag, P. Paradise Lost: California's Experience, *America's Future.* The New Press, 2004.

Starr, K. *Americans and the California Dream*, vols I-VII, 1986-2011. Oxford University Press, 1973.

The Future of California's Workforce. The Institute of Future, 2011. www.iftf.org

GDP PER CAPITA
The World Bank. data.worldbank.org

POPULATION BY RACE
POPULATION BY AGE
US Census. www.census.gov

Report P-2: Population Projections by Race/ Ethnicity and 5-Year Age Groups, 2010-2060. California Department of Finance. www.dof.ca.go

HOW DOES CALIFORNIA COMPARE?
Innovation: Number of Patents, 2012. www.uspto.gov

Renewable Energy: Million kWh. www.census.gov

Agriculture: Net Farm Income, 2011. www.ers.usda.gov

Exports: Value, 2011. www.census.gov

Greenhouse Gas Emissions: Metric CO_2 tons per capita, 2009. www.e3network.org

Income Inequality: Gini coefficient. www.census.gov

Supplemental Poverty Rate: Percentage of Households in Poverty. The Research Supplemental Poverty Measure: 2011. US Census Bureau, November 2012. www.census.gov

Food Insecurity: Percentage of households with food insecurity. www.ers.usda.gov

Education: Expenditure per pupil K-12. Quality Counts, *Edweek*, 2013. www.edweek.org

Health: Percentage of Non-elderly Population Uninsured. California's Uninsured: Treading Water. California Health Care Foundation, 2012. www.chcf.org

CHAPTER 10 DATA CHALLENGES

Hill, L, Johnson HP, Unauthorized Immigrants in California. PPIC, July 2011.

Health Outcome and Health Factors Rankings. Population Health Institute, University of Wisconsin, 2012.

Hanak, E et al. Managing California's Water. PPIC, 2011, pp 330.

California Renewable Energy Statistics and Data, energyalmanac.ca.gov/renewables/index.html [Accessed March 12, 2013]. It states that "in 2009, 11.6% of all electricity came from renewable resources."

Cook, Sherburne F. *The Population of the California Indians: 1769-1970.* University of California Press, 1976.

INDEX